Decision Sourcing

For Lizzie and Ethan

Decision Sourcing

Decision Making for the Agile Social Enterprise

DALE ROBERTS
and
ROOVEN PAKKIRI

Routledge
Taylor & Francis Group

LONDON AND NEW YORK

First published 2013 by Gower Publishing

Published 2016 by Routledge
2 Park Square, Milton Park, Abingdon, Oxfordshire OX14 4RN
711 Third Avenue, New York, NY 10017, USA

First issued in paperback 2016

Routledge is an imprint of the Taylor & Francis Group, an informa business

British Library Cataloguing in Publication Data
Roberts, Dale.
    Decision sourcing : decision making for the agile social enterprise.
    1. Decision making. 2. Social media. 3. Decision support systems.
    I. Title II. Pakkiri, Rooven.
    658.4'03 – dc23

The Library of Congress has cataloged the printed edition as follows:
Roberts, Dale, 1963–
    Decision sourcing : decision making for the agile social enterprise / by Dale Roberts and Rooven Pakkiri.
        p. cm.
    ncludes bibliographical references and index.
    ISBN 978-1-4094-4247-9 (hardback : alk. paper)
1. Decision making. 2. Business intelligence. 3. Social media.
I. Pakkiri, Rooven. II. Title.

    HD30.23.R598 2013
    658.4'03 – dc23

                                                                    2012037712

ISBN 13: 978-1-138-27173-9 (pbk)
ISBN 13: 978-1-4094-4247-9 (hbk)

Contents

List of Figures

List of Tables

About the Authors

Dale Roberts is an executive and co-founder of Artesian Solutions, an innovator in social customer relationship management. Prior to this he advised global businesses on analytics and organisational decision making for more than two decades, one of which was as a European Services Director for the market-leading analytics provider Cognos.

Rooven Pakkiri is a digital evangelist focusing on how social technology is making fundamental changes to the way we think, communicate and work. Rooven runs regular thought leader events and truly innovative digital shows to help companies and individuals to understand social business. He also speaks at industry events on this subject.

Foreword

The corporation is continually evolving. We saw this in the work of Peter Drucker in the 1970s and 1980s, Michael Porter and Robert Kaplan in the 1990s, Gary Hamel in the 2000s, and many other thought leaders before and after. The primary motivation for change is us. As customers, employers and employees, the enterprise reflects our society and our values. The last few decades have seen cultural change and technology transform organisations into global, networked and open enterprises that would be barely recognisable to earlier management thinkers.

There has been no greater disruptive force than the Internet. The dot.com boom and bubble of the 1990s gave way to new ways of working and thinking. What started more than a decade ago with discussions about Enterprise 2.0 has rapidly evolved into a new economic model. Companies can no longer compete in the same way that they used to for customers, talent or brand equity. A new business is emerging – one that engages customers and employees in a genuine two-way dialogue. These businesses are hyper-connected, using technology to link people to people and people to information in unprecedented ways and at previously unimaginable speed and scale.

In my book *Get Bold*, I describe the power shift from process to people. Customers no longer need to take their turn in a customer service line to register their complaint. They can share it in real time with potentially millions of others around the globe. As I write this, many high-profile organisations are paying the price of ignoring social business while others are investing, learning, growing and ultimately reaping the rewards by adapting to this new world of authentic engagement.

Roberts and Pakkiri begin their work with an examination of organisational decision making. They argue that with the rise of social business, these traditional (often hierarchical) processes will transpose to an organic, collaborative approach for forming and delivering company policy. And this trend will be a key driver in achieving business transformation and delivering competitive advantage. The perspective arrived at by the authors is a fascinating one. Roberts's extensive background in analytics combined with Pakkiri's in social provides a unique perspective on the opportunities facing a modern and social business. It provides rigorously researched material for managers and management thinkers into approaches that will continue the trend in social transformation from within.

Like the authors, I am excited about what the future holds.

Read, ponder and enjoy.

Sandy Carter

Sandy Carter is Vice President of Social Business Evangelism, in which capacity she is responsible for helping to set IBM's Social Business initiative, a $200 billion marketplace. Ms Carter is the best-selling author of three books: The New Language of Business: SOA and Web 2.0 *(2007), which won the Platinum MarCom Award in 2008,* The New Language of Marketing 2.0: How to use ANGELS to Energize Your Market *(2009), which won the Silver MarketingSherpa Award in 2009, and* Get Bold: Using Social Media to Create a New Type of Social Business *(2012).*

Preface

The journey that resulted in this book is a case study for what twentieth-century sociologist Robert K. Merton popularised as 'unintended consequence'. It started with an act of open generosity from IBM veteran Colin Chesterman. While on secondment to one of IBM's major distributors, Arrow ECS, Chesterman hosted a series of events which he referred to as 'Partner Jams'. Unusually, given the conservative nature of both of Chesterman's employers, these events had no purpose other than getting completely unrelated business partners in the same room to see what might happen. They were an exercise in facilitated serendipity. The events had more in common with open mic nights or speed dating than with the usual formal meetings associated with global technology vendors. They were more Googleplex, Mountain View than Armonk, New York. In between the occasional hard sells, there were fresh, crisp, improvised introductions to innovations and the people that had bought them to market. There was, on one memorable occasion, even a presentation in poetry. I considered, but quickly dismissed, trying to top this by introducing my own business through the medium of interpretive dance.

Instead, I took a safer option. I shared a view on the future of business intelligence, analytics and decision making. It was opinion and crystal ball stuff. My predictions, though, had solid foundations. They were based on more than a decade of working with customers implementing analytics systems, and specifically where they fell short. Much of what my peers and the analysts were saying echoed what I was hearing from those organisations that were leading the field. The recurring theme was that informed decision making wasn't enough. My customers certainly had data, and in abundance. They also had slick visualisations, charts, dashboards and key performance indicators. Yet there was something missing. My suspicion was that what was missing from organisational decision making was what was missing from many organisations: the human voice. This struck more than a chord with someone else in the room. Rooven Pakkiri took no time in tracking me down after my session finished. Pakkiri had no background in business intelligence and analytics, rather he was a native of the dot.com era, a speaker and Head of Social Business for another IBM business partner. He was somewhat wary of the way in which social (our industry's shorthand for 'social technologies') was being positioned. Up to this point it was chiefly about knowledge sharing, and only had consistent currency with IT departments. This was understandable. In an information economy where knowledge is the fuel on which businesses run, social had many of the answers. The results of early social implementations, though, were not always good. CEO blogs started off enthusiastically enough, but quickly became occasional forums filled with tumbleweed and folksonomies that looked threadbare. In Pakkiri's view, there was something around the corner even more significant, more important, more tangible – Something that would give social some weight. To Pakkiri, social was nothing short of a revolution, and something in what I had shared had sparked an interest in the place where social and analytics met.

A spark, it turns out, was something Pakkiri needed the least. He talked of the social space with urgency and intensity. In turn, he listened intently to my experiences in the business intelligence field. What followed was a series of kinetic meetings to join the dots, and a few short weeks later we were meeting customers together and exploring our ideas. We had built a demo and a presentation to illustrate collaborative decision making. In the background, our companies had engaged an agency to book us meetings with companies that were either already experimenting with collaborative decision making or interested in learning more. The same agency had previously been arranging meetings with companies interested in business intelligence at about the rate of four per month. When we asked them to arrange meetings to discuss social business intelligence, they had arranged ten meetings in the first two weeks. Within six weeks they had arranged 35, and we eventually had to ask them to take a break from calling once we exceeded 50. There were only so many meetings that the two of us could attend. It seemed that the socialisation of business intelligence made sense to everyone our agency spoke with, and they wanted to know more. And they were the great and good of the corporate world, too. We travelled around the UK meeting Arcadia, Disney, McDonald's, ITV, Bupa, HSBC, Rolls-Royce, Office Depot and the London Stock Exchange. It seems that everyone wanted to share their early experiences or hear about the possibilities of delivering business intelligence on a social platform.

And it didn't stop there. Month after month, Pakkiri and I travelled the length and breadth of the UK comparing notes on collaborative decision making with airports, retailers, investment banks, restaurant chains and manufacturers. Time after time we sat through meetings where those responsible for decision support nodded occasionally in the first few minutes and then vigorously in the final few. Meetings scheduled to follow ours were frequently postponed so that we could spend more time debating the vision, drilling into what it might mean for their own organisation. Not that there wasn't a healthy amount of scepticism, too. This was a time when many businesses were trying to find ways to tie up social tools with policies, or even ban them outright. Ultimately, though, while there were challenges, there was no dissent. It made sense. The limitations of time and space were holding back good decisions as much as the quality of information. Something had changed for ever in the corporate body that led the way to better, faster decisions from an engaged and knowledgeable workforce. We were in the middle of a transformation, a revolution. Pakkiri was right all along. You only needed to step back and open your eyes to see it.

Although written from my perspective, the book's origin, development and co-creation is as a result of the countless hours Pakkiri and I have spent with businesses on their collaborative decision making journey. The ideas were honed through frenetic collaboration and excited analysis of our findings in authors' meetings often convened after long days with customers. Like the subject matter itself, it required Pakkiri's perspective on social and mine on analytics to converge into a coherent and convergent form.

There are many people to thank. The first is Robin McNeil, who introduced me to and bewildered me with the prescient notion of social decision making in the 1990s. It was an idea so 'out there' that it took another ten years for me to 'get it'. Jonathan Norman fuelled the project with belief and support while demonstrating inhuman patience at my repeated misuse of the possessive apostrophe. Huw Edwards – no, not that one – helped Rooven and myself to navigate the vast IBM organisation. Mike Blackadder – yes, that's his real name – supported me in my own organisation when I should frankly have been doing something less interesting and more immediate than writing a book about the future of organisational decision making. Peter Taylor, author of *Leading Successful PMOs*, coached me on the writing process. It's more difficult than it looks, but more fun, too. Stephen Few, Mark Madsen, Ben Goldacre, Bill Inmon, Neil Raden and many other leading thinkers who share freely online and on social platforms. Gary Hodsdon, Tally Hatzakis, Will McInnes, Leon Benjamin, Mike Morrison, Simon Collister and my co-author, Rooven Pakkiri, listened to my early unintelligible ramblings and helped me shape them into coherent themes. David Ayling-Smith and Alan Chapman continue to coach me through life with wisdom, humour and grace. Finally, but by no means least, there are my wife Liz and my son Ethan. Anyone who has lived with someone who is writing a book, particularly a first book, will understand the sacrifices that they made.

Dale Roberts

1

Decisions: The Unit of Success

Elizabeth Swann: There will come a time when you have a chance to do the right thing.
Jack Sparrow: I love those moments. I like to wave at them as they pass by.
Keira Knightley and Johnny Depp, Pirates of the Caribbean: Dead Man's Chest, *directed by Gore Verbinski*

An organisation's performance relative to its competitors is no more or less than the sum of the decisions it makes and executes.
Paul Rogers, Michael C. Mankins and Marcia Blenko, Decide and Deliver

---

SIGNPOSTS

✓ The relationship between decision making and organisational success
✓ How our understanding of rationality and decision making is changing
✓ What decision support systems are missing
✓ Why organisational decisions are naturally social

Decision: The Atomic Unit of Success

French author and philosopher Albert Camus once said: 'Life is a sum of all your choices.' This is not an uncommon notion, a familiar construct referenced by Rogers, Mankins and Blenko in *Decide and Deliver* when they suggest that corporate success is the sum of its decisions. Personal and professional choices punctuate our daily life. Many are automatic, unconscious, based on a model of principles and preferences – the clothes we choose to wear, the drink at the coffee shop, the car parking spot, those emails we respond to and those we junk – all without much thought. Others are conscious and considered – the hiring decisions, annual salary reviews or the right level of discount that will hopefully win a deal. Some are difficult, perhaps even a source of anxiety and stress because of their importance and their impact on us and those around us. In any situation that requires our determination because time, money and resources are constrained – which is to say always – decisions need to be made. Decisions require judgement. The choice between two suppliers, indistinct in every respect with the exception of pricing, is a question of mathematics. The absence of judgement makes it a calculation, not a decision. These are easy. Decisions are those things we fear getting wrong. Many sleepless nights have been spent deciding which plants to close down when revenues have inescapably declined. Many have been preoccupied by the decision of which multi-million-dollar opportunities they should direct their busy and expensive bid teams at.

Organisational decisions are, in a sense, no different to personal decisions. While they are made on behalf of and in the interest of a separate entity – the company – they are made by people, sometimes individually, sometimes in groups. It is perhaps this that makes them frequently unpredictable, sometimes irrational, and occasionally capricious – a logical business process with human characteristics. We believe that decisions should be the outcome of a reasoned and rational process. They are the product of considering a set of alternatives, predicting the outcome of each alternative, assessing the value of each outcome, and deciding using a set of rules by which these values are measured. Cold, hard and logical. Infallible. Except that organisational decision making is evidently fallible.

Decision Making, the Fallible Process

Many well-informed, deeply experienced and well-educated individuals decided to invest in and securitise subprime mortgage loans. Others decided to hedge risk with credit default swaps. Those who did this for Kaupthing and Lehman Brothers bet their companies, and lost. This was catastrophic decision making on a global scale across a whole industry, but individual businesses more regularly make eyewateringly poor decisions. Yahoo! turned down an offer from Microsoft in 2008 that was worth $44 billion. The offer was, at one point, worth over $30 a share – more than twice the value of the shares in 2012 as the organisation announces more layoffs. Stephen Russell, CEO of Boots, the UK's second most trusted retailer, introduced dentistry and chiropody into Boots stores as Boots Wellbeing Services. The enterprise lost £100 million, and it cost a further £50 million to re-convert the space back to retail. It resulted in 700 job losses, including Russell's own. These are smart people in great companies with access to more resources, more capital and more information than most. The list is long. General Motors, British Petroleum, Toyota, the entire music industry have all made sometimes questionable, sometimes disastrous decisions. Even Apple had its 'Antennagate'. Still, this didn't stop it taking lunch money and market share from Sony, Research In Motion and Nokia, which seemingly decided to do little to stop it.

Organisational decision making is flawed. For all their scale, their access to the best people and investment in the latest tools, corporations still leave important decisions largely to individuals. The result can be poor decisions made without rigour and their outcomes left unscrutinised. Not all alternatives are discovered, not all outcomes considered, and decision rules are applied inconsistently. Relevant information about alternatives is not always sought, and even what information is available is not always used. In short, what should be methodical and logical is not. Organisational decision makers try to be rational, but they cannot be – at least not always. They are constrained, they are bounded, they are human. Recently human limitations of rationality have become generally accepted through the work of behavioural economists like Dan Ariely in his book *Predictably Irrational* and by Richard Thaler and Cass Sunstein in their book *Nudge*. Ariely, for example, observes that given the choice of a holiday to Paris with free breakfast, Rome with free breakfast or Rome without breakfast, the most popular choice will consistently involve breakfast in St Peter's Square. The reason? It is easier to compare the two options in Rome than it is to subjectively compare Rome and Paris.

Organisational decision making, characteristically involving others, makes this an order of magnitude more complex. James G. March, Professor Emeritus at Stanford University, highly respected for his research on organisational decision making, describes a series of problems specific to organisational decisions in his book *A Primer on Decision Making*. March outlines how the notion of *limited rationality* is considered an extension to the *theory of rationality* by its enthusiasts, and a challenge by its sceptics. Limited rationality applies both to humans as individuals and to the collection of individuals that is an organisation. There are problems of attention and time because both are limited in people. There are problems of memory because of the biological limitations of people and organisational limits of physical storage and retrieval. There are also problems of comprehension because decision makers sometimes have difficulty organising, summarising and using information to form inferences and patterns. They might have relevant information but fail to see its relevance or its connection. Finally, there are problems of communication because there are limited capacities for sharing complex and specialised information across corporate silos.

Decision Making Poverty

It was studying March's work along with that of Herbert Simon that started off a chain of events which resulted in the collaboration between Pakkiri and myself, and later the development of this book. The systems used by businesses today for improving decision making are almost exclusively about delivering information. Analytic applications and business intelligence (BI) systems are evolutions of executive information systems (EIS) and decision support systems (DSS) before them. They all aim to improve business outcomes through improving organisational decision making, and they all improve organisational decision making by making them more informed. In spite of decades of research that suggest that when organisational decisions fail, they do so as a result of limited attention, time, memory, comprehension and communication, businesses believe that they can arrive at the best possible decisions simply by surrounding themselves with more information. It isn't that decisions don't need to be informed; they do. However, in the era of so-called 'Big Data', an age when it is within the practical reach of businesses to know all that there is to know, do we really think that the result will be perfect decision making? Pakkiri named this phenomenon the 'poverty of corporate decision making'. Outside reports, scorecards, dashboards and charts, it is narrowly defined, poorly understood, casually overlooked and receives scant management or systems attention.

Social: The Missing Piece

It soon became apparent that what was missing from systematic organisational decision making was already a growing phenomenon in the world of business systems and corporate culture. Referred to as 'Enterprise 2.0' by authors like Niall Cook and Harvard's Andrew McAfee, we were witnessing an explosion in what many refer to as 'social media'. The phenomenon, while wholly remarkable, had been most notable in the world of marketing. Platforms like Facebook, approaching a billion users, saw people gather into communities in a way that was unprecedented. Rather than this being a new 'channel' for broadcasting, enlightened marketers saw it as an opportunity to engage in conversations and to build something more meaningful than a sale, a discount or a deal – a relationship. Social is a state of mind as much as it is a category of software – more so. Nor is it just about the relationship between business and customer. Those with whom companies are forging new forms of relationship are also the same people that come to work each morning. 'Social' has become a prefix not just to 'sales' and 'marketing', but also to 'customer services', 'HR' and 'operations'. 'Social' is a term rapidly on its way to becoming fleetingly ubiquitous, then redundant. The cultural shift that is social is changing the way businesses do business.

Social adoption inside the organisation has, so far, been patchy. Readily adopted by those keen to collaborate around IT projects, it has gracefully became part of the technologists' tool kit and working practices. Platforms like Microsoft's Sharepoint or Google Drive make it easy to join forces around a document, spreadsheet, presentation, project plan or software sprint. Elsewhere, though, it was being treated with caution, even suspicion. While it promised the democratisation of content, even knowledge through simple tools like blogs, wikis and activity streams, take-up has been tentative thus far. One of the reasons, perversely, is precisely because social behaves the way people do. It aligns closely to our interactions, our working patterns, our habits. And habits change slowly. Many 'failed' social implementations did not fail at all. They just hadn't been given enough time. Regardless of early failures, the rise of enterprise social is now inevitable. In the 2012 Global CEO Study *Leading Through Connections* from IBM, only 16 per cent of CEOs said that they used social to engage customers today, but they also expected their use to triple in the next five years. The study of over 1,700 CEOs provides insights into the cultural shift, too. It urges organisations to replace the rulebook with beliefs, to behave consistently with their values and to eliminate unnecessary controls. None of these are overnight changes, but they point to the rise of the social enterprise, one where the pervasive adoption of social practices, principles and technologies has fundamentally changed the relationships with their customers, staff and partners.

Better Decisions

One of the nascent but profound benefits to emerge from this cultural and technological shift is collaborative decision making. The process of gathering and communicating information to arrive at a shared insight for the purpose of making a decision was previously slow and complex. Involving all but a limited group was impractical. Social tools are eliminating cultural and organisational barriers so that more decisions can involve more people more of the time. They address problems of attention and time, problems of sharing and retrieving. They bring people together in such a way that they can co-operatively solve problems. They revolutionise the way people share information and communicate. Industry analysts like Gartner and Forrester have already made their predictions. James Kobielus of Forrester, in his article 'Predictions for Business Analytics in 2011' for *InformationWeek*, saw performance management 'evolving rapidly towards a more social architecture'. Gartner predicts that by the time this book is published in 2013, a significant minority of analytic deployments will already be attempting to combine collaboration, BI and social software into a single decision making environment. As William Gibson once said, 'The future is already here, it is just not very evenly distributed.' The predictions have been made, the scene has been set, the convergence of social and BI declared greater than the sum of their parts. This is what organisational decision making and performance management have been waiting for: decisions that scale; better decisions through human collaboration.

Decision Sourcing: **What to Expect**

Our intention in this book is to share our journey so far and to:

- help you understand why it is that social tools have had a disproportionate impact on our personal rather than our professional lives, and most importantly, why this is about to change;

- illustrate how entrenched corporate cultures and expensive company systems are being challenged by social;

- show how corporate information, in fact the very nature of knowledge, is changing;

- predict what new, previously impossible insights social tools will offer;

- explain why hierarchy and status impede decisions, and why the new era of networked decisions will help organisations become and stay agile;

- demonstrate that organisations can surpass the limited and bounded nature of individual decision making rather than be limited by it;

- introduce a whole new listening framework – the foundation of a social enterprise;

- prove that there is a practical and real alternative to control and bureaucracy;

- challenge conventional wisdom by explaining how inclusive decision making will speed up rather than slow down businesses, making them more, not less, competitive.

2

BYO

To traditional corporations, networked conversations may appear confused, may sound confusing. But we are organizing faster than they are. We have better tools, more new ideas, no rules to slow us down.

Chris Locke et al., The Cluetrain Manifesto, *Thesis 94*

SIGNPOSTS

- ✓ How social tools impact our lifestyles
- ✓ Why social crosses the divide between work and home
- ✓ Why we no longer accept systems that are 'user-friendly'
- ✓ The nature of knowledge sharing and decision making

We Have Better Tools

The internationally acclaimed book *The Cluetrain Manifesto*, published in 2000, contained 95 theses with which the authors Christopher Lock, Doc Searls, David Weinberger and Rick Levine described the new reality of a networked world where the authentic human voice drowns out corporate marketing messages. The first thesis, 'markets are conversations', encapsulates the essence of this change so succinctly that it continues to be a recurring mantra in books, blogs and many other texts today. The 94th thesis is far less frequently quoted, but has proven almost prophetic. It claims that people, not corporations, will have better tools, and that this, along with an absence of bureaucracy, will mean that they will be better organised.

In 2012, a full thirteen years after *The Cluetrain Manifesto* was first published, one of these tools, Facebook, had reached around one billion users. The microblogging service Twitter reported, that it had two hundred million active users. That's more than 1.4 million users for each one of their 140 character limit. Both services were appearing frequently in the news precisely because of their capacity to organise people. The timing of a series of protests and demonstrations in the Arab world that started at the end of 2010 and ran well into the following year, known as the 'Arab Spring', was attributed to the widespread availability of both Twitter and Facebook. This was a revolution in the truest sense – civil unrest that resulted in the fall of the Libyan government and the resignation of the Yemeni prime minister. Even those who felt that the role of social tools was being overstated by the press conceded that social networking had played a significant role. In a *Telegraph* article in July 2011, Man Booker Prize-shortlisted author Hisham Matar expressed his irritation at the exaggeration, but conceded that social networking sites had provided 'a vital means of communication'. A 2012 study by Zizi Papacharissi and Maria de Fatima Oliveira of the University of Illinois of 1.5 millions tweets with the #Egypt hashtag during 25 January–25 February 2011 explained more about the use of social in the uprising. The study, itself a brand-new possibility, concluded that social media use had unique features. The first was the drama of the immediate: events being reported instantly increase the desire to read and share. The second was the existence of a crowdsourced elite: activists rose to prominence through re-tweets and replies. The third was solidarity: expressions of support and encouragement came from within Egypt, but also globally. Finally, it was a never-ending news source that was always on, organic and had its own rhythm. While there was some sensationalism, social tools were clearly altering the nature of social organisation, as well as the speed and efficiency with which people were able to organise themselves.

The business world, however, was slow to grasp the implications of tools that helped groups connect and organise themselves efficiently and purposefully. Instead, some concluded that they would be a distraction or a risk to the corporate reputation rather than spurring a productivity boon. According to a 2011 survey of 2,500 companies by Lewis Communications and HCL Technologies,[1] almost half of companies prevented their workers using Facebook and Twitter. This demonstrated a level of mistrust, but also misunderstanding. By 2011 a growing number of posts were made through mobile devices completely beyond the reach of corporate policy.

While some HR departments were developing or refining policies to prevent social tools being used at work, those whom the policy targeted were continuing to use their 'better tools'. They shared what they were thinking or

---

1   http://blog.lewispr.com/2011/05/are-you-still-banning-twitter-and-facebook-at-work.html.

doing while they rode the train, queued for a cappuccino or, at some risk to their personal safety, while they walked the final few yards from the coffee shop to the office. This required so little effort that much of it was conducted on mobile devices with small, sometimes awkward, on-screen keyboards without any real difficulty. These same devices rendered the policies unenforceable. Executives couldn't see beyond the informal, sometimes trivial nature of these updates to the thousands of use cases for them in their businesses. They could not see that the tools that allowed their staff to connect to each other in unprecedented ways in their personal lives had the potential to dramatically improve the way in which they connected in the workplace.

Let me offer a personal example. I recently updated my Facebook status with a holiday picture – just one. It was a picture of my wife and myself underwater in Bonaire in the Dutch Antilles. Our Dive Master had take the photograph at about 10 metres at a dive site just a few kilometres south of the capital, Kralendijk, where an old ship had been sunk and had settled at around 15 metres. It was a great picture. The masks and breathing regulators couldn't hide our smiles or how happy and relaxed we were. As a usually anxious diver, it summed up the holiday for me, so I was happy to post it. The effort it required on my part was minimal. I attached and posted the picture in just four steps (Add Photo, Upload Photo, Choose File, Select File). It required so little effort that I invested some time in giving it what I thought was an amusing title. Over the next few days close friends and family posted comments. Some commented on comments. Others who didn't have the time or motivation to comment clicked a single button to let me know that they had seen it and liked it. When I look back now, I can see a record of that picture with all those comments arranged neatly underneath it. Comments on comments are indented so that there is a general sense of what friends thought about the picture. A conversational tangent, perhaps on coral bleaching, need not distract from the overall flow, but can be expanded and read thoroughly if other friends are interested.

Compare this with a piece of work I needed to complete shortly after I returned from holiday. I engaged a graphic designer to create a single-page document that visually represented our businesses key products and services. When I received the first draft, I needed to share the document with colleagues and gather their feedback for the designer to iterate the final document. I had received the draft by email, so I used email to set about the task in hand. First, I had to decide with whom in our business it should be shared, and assign them to the 'To' list. From these people, I expected feedback. Then I decided who was to be on the 'Copy' list. Their input was optional, or they just needed to be kept informed because I had engaged a supplier and was incurring costs. Once I had assembled the lists, I attached the document, typed my request for feedback and sent the email. I almost immediately received a couple of out of office replies, so I made a mental note that it would be a little over a week before I could expect feedback from everyone. I did receive some feedback within the hour, and more drifted in over the next few days, mostly solid and constructive. One of the suggested changes I politely rejected because the reviewer hadn't really taken into account the intended audience for the finished document. This resulted in a tangential dialogue over the course of two or three emails to clarify and finally explain why the changes would not be included. Some of my colleagues Replied All, some did not, and in any case the email thread quickly became fragmented, so I followed up with a second email to summarise the feedback. I knew this would be just an interim summarisation, and sure enough, it became out of date almost the moment it left my outbox as comments came in from colleagues returning from being out of the office. I sent what I hoped would be a final summary, but made the mistake of leaving it open to final comments. The whole process circled around one more time, but with fewer comments in a fourth email before I finally went back to my graphics designer with a list of amendments. Managing this task with forty-year-old technology meant that the exercise took more than 20 steps – five times that of my holiday picture, and many of the individual steps also took longer. There was no single, organised record of this set of interactions. My summarisation came close, but it had taken a lot of effort, and we still each had a slightly different set of conversations in our email inboxes. As I passed the final set of feedback to the graphic designer late one evening, I sighed again at the extra effort required to do something in my work life that I was able to do much more easily in my personal life. I wanted to take my better tools to work.

BYO (Bring Your Own)

It seems that in 2012, I was far from alone. Perhaps only a year after the Lewis/ HCL study, another, *How Social Technologies Drive Business Success* from Google and Millward Brown, a leading global research agency, showed a prominent shift. Out of 2,700 professionals questioned, almost three quarters of senior managers were using social tools at least once a week. Interestingly, one third of this sample were still using external social tools such as Facebook, Google+ and Twitter for work-related purposes rather than tools set up specifically for use within the business (enterprise social tools). This demonstrated that while businesses were becoming more open-minded to social tools and relaxing their corporate polices, they were still not always investing in corporate equivalents. The response from professionals already convinced that social tools would impact business strategy, help businesses to grow more rapidly, increase productivity and attract the best people was to bring their own. Unprepared to wait any longer for corporate IT to keep up, they introduced the tools they used in their personal life to their professional life.

Businesses are dealing with the unstoppable consumerisation of IT. The lines between work and personal life are all but gone. The office is at home, not just at work. Business documents are stored in cloud-based services like Dropbox, SugarSync and Google Drive rather than the company network, and teleconferences across time zones will include at least one worker still in their pyjamas. Work now takes place in our personal space, so we want to choose the tools with which we work. Tablets and smartphones are replacing laptops and desktops. In fact, according to Forrester in their 2012 Forrsights workforce employee survey, sixty per cent of devices are used by information workers for both work and personal purposes. What is true of devices is true of the applications, too. The Google/Millward Brown survey suggested that the same three-quarters using social tools believed that they would change the way businesses operate in the future, that they have enabled them to be more efficient, and that the businesses that embrace them will grow more quickly than those that don't. Those who are using social tools are seeing an impact on their careers, too. Almost 90 per cent of frequent users of social tools had recently been promoted. The evidence suggests that the benefits to them and to their businesses were too great to wait. In many cases they didn't hold on for their IT team to implement social tools. They brought their own.

Frictionless

So what was it that made my experience with my holiday photograph so efficient and my experience with my marketing document so much less so? There are a number of principles at play. The tool I used to share my holiday photograph was specifically designed and built to allow social groups – two or more humans with a common interest – to interact. Prior to the introduction of social tools, business systems focused on processing financial and operational transactions while office automation focused on automating documents, spreadsheets and email messages. In fact, the humble calendar program introduced us to what we believe was the first widely adopted social tool: the meeting request.

Before the meeting request, it required what could be an almost endless stream of email messages among a group of people to identify a common diary slot when all could attend. In arriving at a mutually agreeable date, the group would exchange messages that offered dates, declined dates, suggested alternatives and provided insights into why some were available while others were not. Contingent offers, perhaps offering a time slot if the meeting could be shortened or conducted in a different location, would exponentially increase the number of messages, forcing the organiser to circle around several times before arriving at a date in the diary. It was small wonder that this task was often delegated to a personal assistant. The meeting request took a common social interaction – inviting one or more people to meet – and automated many of the micro-interactions within it. Declaring guests as optional or mandatory, proposing alternative times, accepting, declining and even tentatively accepting were all automated interactions rather than messages, and they were all tracked so that the organiser could immediately check whether the meeting could go ahead or whether a little more planning was required. We perhaps didn't appreciate how much interaction the meeting request was automating for us, but this curious but elegant artifact of the desktop age pointed to a new class of tools that would help us to conduct any work that required interaction more efficiently. I am convinced that one of the reasons for early executive resistance to social tools is because they are called 'social'. Social is what people do at the bar, restaurant, cinema or football stadium. It isn't what they do at work. The term 'social' is spectacularly misleading in this context. It isn't the adjective that describes the act of going out and enjoying activities outside work. It is attributive. It relates to society or organisation. Businesses are, like all social structures, organised around a common purpose – one of economic activity. Social tools automate group-forming, status updates, sharing, collaboration and many other forms of interaction that are as relevant in the workplace as they are at home.

Some of the interactions with my friends and family over my holiday photograph were so highly automated, so efficient that they mirrored human social gestures. Imagine you're in a restaurant – an expensive one, as it's imaginary. You're talking to your friend, and mid-sentence, she places her index finger to her slightly pursed lips. What do you do? I would imagine you would immediately lower your voice. You might or might not finish off what you were saying before enquiring why your friend felt you needed to be quieter. However, if in the middle of the same conversation she held her hand outstretched, mid-way across the table, flat towards your face, you would stop, possibly even mid-word. Both of these social gestures are highly abbreviated forms of human communication. In fact, one of the most universally useful social gestures will be used right at the end of the evening. Pinching your thumb and forefinger together as if holding a pen followed by a short, circular or flourished wave in the air while catching the eye of your waiter will almost always result in your receiving a large bill. This gesture is so commonly used that it will work even if you're not multilingual and your imaginary restaurant is in Paris, Rome or Frankfurt. Human social gestures are shaped by culture, history and collective memory. They can reduce a lengthy conversation to a single signal, and they are an integral component of social tools. With a single gesture or click, it is possible to 'like' a document 'rate' its value or 'share' its content. Let's take another universal human gesture: lifting a single thumb in the air to signify our approval. A single click on a thumbs-up icon communicates the same message as adding the comment 'I like this,' but it's easier. It's a single click rather than two clicks and nine keystrokes. The difference in ease of use is marginal, but it removes what is a very low barrier to participation. In the absence of the 'like' gesture, many of my friends and family would have not felt motivated enough to offer thoughts or comments in the same way that when you meet a group of people that you haven't met for a while some will express how pleased they are to see you again and others will shake your hands and smile in a way that a similar message has been communicated.

In 2010, YouTube, host a billion video views every day, changed its rating system. The existing system allowed each of the videos to be graded with one to five stars. What YouTube discovered, though, is that the vast majority of votes were either one star or five stars. Those who interacted with the content determined whether the video was good or bad, but were simply not prepared to invest the time in any finer analysis and grading. In a connected world where there is so much that demands the attention of individuals with a hard and fast 24 hours each day, people will instinctively decide how much they are prepared to invest in an interaction. What YouTube discovered was the precise level of effort its consumers were prepared to invest, and it was very small. YouTube viewers were prepared to 'like', but unprepared to rate the content they viewed. Initially, social gestures were limited to a small number of lightweight activities, including 'liking'. The future will see the addition of new gestures that will tell us more about the way individuals are interacting with one another. For example, one social platform implemented a 'used' gesture. It's shorthand for 'I liked this document so much that I used it and it worked for me, too.'

By adding a 'Like' button and identifying a common interaction within the universe of interactions we can isolate, capture, analyse and make further use of it. It's life-affirming to know how many friends and family liked my photograph, but there would also be practical and productivity implications if I had used a social tool to share my marketing document. I could have captured how many liked it and whether there were any dislikes that could potentially veto the whole document. The final document would also be rated, it might even become highly 'used', and therefore, rather than sitting unnoticed on a hard drive somewhere, it might get picked up by colleagues who were not on the immediate distribution list and who might have missed it had it not been flagged as useful by so many others.

Ubiquitous Computing and the Ubiquitous Network

The carefree and casual ease with which my holiday picture was shared and commented on was also made possible because computing is out of the server room, off of my desktop, and exists where I live. It is everywhere. It is ubiquitous. Well almost. We are living through the beginning of the third age of computing, or what Alan Kay of Apple calls 'the third paradigm'. The first was the mainframe – large, imposing, wardrobe-sized computers affordable only to large businesses which gave their staff access to them through dumb terminals. Then came personal computing, characterised by the rise of the PC and Microsoft. It is no coincidence that the overriding metaphor in the Windows operating system is the desktop, because this era put computing on every desk in every office, as well as on desks in studies, bedrooms and dining rooms in many homes. The next era was first built as 'tabs', 'pads' and 'boards' at the distinguished research company Xerox PARC during 1988–94. It illustrated that while mainframes gave us one computer for many people and desktops offered one computer per person, ubiquitous computing meant that each person had many computers, or rather computing devices with a variety of uses. IBM refers to this phenomenon as being 'instrumented'. Mark Weiser, regarded as the originator of ubiquitous computing, predicted that it required mobility, or what he referred to as 'nomadicity', wireless connectivity and the Internet as a 'backbone'. Weiser's terminology may not have fallen into common usage but modern devices are often mobile. They are also increasingly aware through geographic location services, accelerometers and other sensors that can literally see and hear their environment. The point of ubiquitous computing though is that it is computing on human terms. The use of computing power is so accessible, so easy, so natural that it becomes an indispensable and invisible part of our lives. So it was with my holiday picture. The picture was taken on a waterproof camera which wirelessly connected to a laptop. The picture was uploaded and could immediately be viewed on my laptop, desktop, phone and tablet, all wirelessly connected to the Internet. My friends and family were on the same network and had access to the same ubiquitous computing with which they effortlessly interacted with me. In the future, ubiquitous computing and networks will extend beyond computing between people (person-to-person) and computing between people and their devices (person-to-object). It will unite everyday objects in one singular network – what is referred to as the 'Internet of things'. In a world of pervasive computing, everyday objects will become both sources and beneficiaries of information. Medicine bottles will issue reminders and even alert carers if patients appear too unwell to follow their regimen. Cars will communicate with the systems of an insurance company to transmit acceleration and braking data. The insurance systems would analyse and assess driving behaviour and then dynamically adjust premiums based on how safely or dangerously the driver was acting.

Single-Instance Sharing

When someone in your network changes job they will probably send you an email with their new details. If you apply the approach of David Allen, author of *Getting Things Done*, to personal productivity then you would determine that this will take less than two minutes to action, switch into your contact management software, update the contact and then delete or file their email. Those that are not David Allen devotees may leave it for later and some will simply forget. Each individual in our mover's network is maintaining their own personal copy of contact details, so the largest number of people in the group are maintaining information with the greatest amount of effort and the least likelihood that they will all remain accurate and up to date. Connected social tools such as LinkedIn are making it possible for one version, a single instance of a contact to exist. Individuals maintain their own details while everyone else shares them through the ubiquitous network.

The manuscript for this book was developed on multiple devices. Whilst most of the writing needed a full keyboard and therefore a laptop computer, some editing was carried out on a tablet, some even on a smartphone. The manuscript was never copied, synchronised or moved. The word processing software was not installed on any of these devices either. The software and manuscript both lived entirely on the centralised hardware and storage of service providers accessible through the ubiquitous network. They lived 'in the cloud'. Single-instance software and documents shared across devices or shared with other people are always up to date, always the latest version and require least effort to keep them that way.

The ubiquitous network makes it theoretically possible to maintain a single copy of software, a contact, a video, a document or any piece of unique information and share access through a system of references, pointers or links. This is single-instance sharing. Single-instance is reducing the cost of software maintenance, minimising storage costs and simplifying digital distribution. However, the implications for single-instance sharing are far more wide-ranging than storage efficiencies. Take for example what is known as the *commodity technology stack*. The commodity technology stack is a large and growing collection of open software tools and utilities. Developers can use these, usually without commercial consideration, to build new software solutions. Solutions to specific problems need only be solved once, committed to the *stack* then freely exploited by the software development community. This is digital sharing that results in single-instance problem-solving.

Single-instance changes the economics of sharing to a point where entire communities, some small, some large, some global can benefit from the actions of a few at least cost to everyone.

Conclusion

The 94th thesis of *The Cluetrain Manifesto* has proven to be remarkably prescient. 'We' have better tools than 'they' do – a billion of us, in any case. It is ironic that many companies started out by limiting access to, or even banning the use of, Facebook at work. The rapid adoption of social tools in our personal lives, though, has trivialised them to the point where every executive has heard a variation on the urban myth that a 'friend' updated their status with 'drinking tea' or 'eating a biscuit'. The reason why most executives underestimate social tools is what makes them most potent. They automate interactions. Until the introduction of social tools, businesses were focused almost entirely on process and transactions. Coincidentally, both workers and customers have grown weary of being account holders, passengers and consumers. They are demanding meaningful interaction, and they are saying so with the very same tools that businesses are banning. The traditional media cannot decide whether they should demonise or dramatise the importance of social tools, but their ability to organise groups is inarguable. The power behind social tools is their ability to deal with human groups, human interactions, across a network that has become as ubiquitous as the computing devices they use to connect.

3

Transaction to Interaction

What a peculiar civilisation this was: inordinately rich, yet inclined to accrue its wealth through the sale of some astonishingly small and only distantly meaningful things, a civilisation torn and unable sensibly to adjudicate between the worthwhile ends to which money might be put and the often morally trivial and destructive mechanisms of its generation.

Alain de Botton, The Pleasures and Sorrows of Work

SIGNPOSTS

- ✓ What businesses miss in the relentless pursuit of process and efficiency
- ✓ Our dissatisfaction with being defined economically as workers and consumers
- ✓ Why systems must reflect the shift from transaction to interaction
- ✓ What's next after knowledge sharing for social tools

The Process World

Prior to the eighteenth century most of the things we needed in everyday life were handmade. A craftsman would take raw materials and produce a candlestick, saddle or pair of shoes from beginning to end, and then trade them at a local market. Over the course of the eighteenth and nineteenth centuries the far-reaching social and economic changes that we now refer to as the Industrial Revolution completely changed this. One of the most significant shifts involved breaking up the process of, for example, wheel-making into smaller activities to improve productivity. In 1776 the Scottish economist and social philosopher Adam Smith described how output in a pin factory was increased through the division of labour in his famous work, the title of which is commonly abbreviated to *Wealth of Nations*. Smith observed that a factory where one man 'draws out the wire', another 'straights it', a third 'cuts it' and a fourth 'points it' might produce tens of thousands of pins a day, whereas a pin factory where each worker produces a pin from start to finish would produce 'very few'. The specialisation of labour was the origin of the business process and the birth of the *process world*. Farmers and artisans didn't live in the process world. They had no need for structured tasks, methods and interfaces. Hatters, potters and blacksmiths concerned themselves with making better hats, pots and tools. Discussions about how they did it were limited to passing on their craft to an apprentice rather than on refining the steps involved in order to increase profit. If they found themselves with what we today call a 'rush order', then they would enlist the help of a journeyman, the equivalent of a temporary worker who had the right skills to help them. Productivity improvements came through an extra pair of hands. However, the efficient management of interdependent tasks in the manufacturing processes that produce a pin or a pot became a new source of economic value. Process engineering in the process world became indispensable, and in large and complex businesses a focus for improvements that would underpin growth and competitive edge. The process world required new disciplines and specialisations that extended way beyond the manufacturing process. The company was transformed over the twentieth century into one that created entirely new disciplines that shaped the modern company into human resources, finance, operations and sales and marketing departments. By the late twentieth century a third of the global labour force were not even involved in manufacturing or agriculture, they were involved in something that would furrow the brow of a furrier – 'service industry'.

In the process world, bewilderingly complex things like designing, manufacturing, marketing, shipping and selling, say, a smartphone are broken down into many smaller processes and co-ordinated and managed in such a way that we can open up a beautifully designed box and find a piece of technology that has journeyed through many thousands, perhaps tens of thousands, of processes.

Systems and Transactions

The unremitting objective of the process world, unchanged since Adam Smith first observed it, is to maximise efficiency. Efficiency results in competitive advantage, reduced costs, improved customer service, or perhaps all three.

The time it takes to conduct an activity – the process cycle time – must be continuously reduced and wasteful exceptions eliminated. Six Sigma, an approach developed by Motorola in the 1980s, aims to drive out exceptions to a point where 99.99966 per cent of products are free of defects – that's 3.4 per million. There is no place for decisions in the process world. Decisions require reflection, an assessment of the situation, an analysis of possible solutions, and a judgement on which one is most likely to offer the best results. All of this slows down the process world. It's friction in a machine that is looking to be well-oiled and frictionless. There is, however, an important place for systems. Systems – and specifically computer systems – automate the process world and have been a weapon by which businesses can wage war on their competitors. New systems improve processes in such a way that a business can do something more profitably than its competitors or even something its competitors cannot do at all. Computer systems introduced in the 1970s and accelerated by the introduction of the Internet in the 1990s that allowed data and funds to be transferred between businesses brought about a period of unprecedented disruptive commercial change and introduced new global corporate giants, including Google, eBay and Amazon. There has now been more than five decades of computer systems evolution in automating business processes inside and outside the corporate headquarters that has resulted in the widespread adoption of enterprise resource planning (ERP) systems. In the process world, ERP systems are a global transport system, automating the flow of business processes. Specific systems control internal processes like manufacturing, finance and human resources. Other ERP systems like customer relationship management (CRM) and supply chain management (SCM) manage processes that extend outside the organisation. At key points, these ERP systems capture the state of the process as a transaction. When an item is received from a supplier, it is captured with a goods received note; when a product is requested by a customer, it is recorded with an order; when it is sent to the customer, it is accompanied by a dispatch note, and when all of this is completed, the customer is billed with an invoice – the font of all corporate revenue. All of these transactions are electronic versions of what were all originally paper documents that ticker taped the important milestones between a business receiving raw materials from its suppliers and cash from a customer.

The Fall of the Transaction

By the beginning of the twenty-first century the process world had evolved into one of exemplary efficiency. Wasteful, repetitive or error-prone processes had been, or were soon to be, re-engineered, outsourced, offshored or eliminated.

The problem, though, was that people don't think or behave like processes. As more and more businesses rolled out CRM systems, it became increasingly apparent that there was a growing dissatisfaction with the process world. The upward trend in CRM systems correlated with the downward trend in customer satisfaction. This is perhaps surprising, until you consider that the primary purpose of these new systems was to provide accurate insights into what customers thought about them. The other, less obvious, reason is that it took the process outside the organisation and forced itself on the customer. Being the subject of a process is objectifying rather than humanising, and while employees were paid to live in the process world customers weren't. They didn't see any reason to accept being marched through someone else's selling process. In fact, it seemed supremely one-sided to refer to a 'sales' cycle. Surely it's a 'buying' cycle. In fact, customers weren't even sure they liked being dealt with in a 'cycle'. Once the customer had been 'closed', they were subjected to more processes – customer services or customer support ones that included automated messages assuring them that their call was important. A colleague and I were debating the reasons why a single tweet resulted in his broadband provider stepping up to the plate, whereas weeks of telephone calls to its support desk had failed. It wasn't that much of a mystery. His calls to Customer Services were private. Safe in this knowledge, his provider could force him through its tortuous internal processes in its own sweet time. His call was important to it, but as a professional blogger with 40,000 followers, his tweet was open, public and damaging. Once it left his iPhone, the clock (or clock app) was ticking. It was a race to respond before other customers, prospective customers and competitors did. This business noticed how its processes were not customer-centric when its customer became better-organised and more vocal on social platforms. And, of course, he was unconstrained by the same systems and processes. When customers started voting with their feet, businesses took a long, hard look at their systems and conceded that they had been built from their own perspective. Louis Gerstner, CEO of IBM from 1993 until 2002, articulated the problem at a major conference and exposition over a decade earlier – in fact, in the winter of 2001. He told business leaders that they needed to focus on interaction rather than transaction. Gerstner was quoted as saying that the 'technology was easy' – presumably if you hired IBM to help you – but more importantly, that 'the hard part is re-conceptualising management models'. This tends to resonate on a personal level, too. Like Patrick McGoohan's character in the 1960s British television series *The Prisoner*, none of us like being a number. We don't like processes, we don't like being systematised. Business systems poured like water but set like concrete, and ignored personal and human interaction. It didn't matter how efficient the transaction became, it wasn't interaction.

Action, Transaction and Interaction

Gerstner's distinction between interaction and transaction was as incisive as he was respected, and the phrase 'transaction to interaction' gained traction. It became synonymous with improving customer service in spite of its broader implication that businesses were not only transacting with their customers, destroying customer satisfaction, they were transacting with their staff, leaving them cold and disengaged. Communication inside and outside a business during the era of the process was fragmented, stilted and inauthentic. It wasn't just the unscrupulous or unprincipled business that was not 'straight' with its customers either. It became the norm for businesses to 'position' and 'message' to represent the business or brand in the best possible light, rather than engaging in honest dialogue. In 2009 Domino's Pizza was forced into a more open relationship with its customers after employees posted a video on YouTube which portrayed what can only be described as public health violations. It was disastrous. Traditional marketing and messaging was not going to deal with the enormous damage inflicted by just two rogue staff. After a shaky start, Domino's engaged with its customers honestly and openly. It launched a series of self-critical ads and ultimately launched new products as part of a 'turnaround' campaign in both traditional and social media. Later, it commendably opted out of the practice of 'food styling'. Domino's CEO Sam Fauser explained that up to 150 people may work on a 30-second pizza commercial, sometimes screwing pizzas to the cutting board, enlisting a hand model to hold it and a stylist to make it look beautiful. That's right, you read correctly, a food stylist. Fauser committed that in future they would use their own pizzas made by an employee and without artificial manipulation. When the process world failed, when transactional marketing couldn't repair its reputation, Domino's was left with no alternative other than to be authentic.

The corporate journey from inauthenticity to authenticity can be illuminated by looking at the evolution of CRM through the lens of information science. Information science is a discipline that concerns itself with the retrieval and dissemination of organisational information along with the way people interact and collaborate around it. A 1973 paper by William F. Eadie at Purdue University, Indiana, based on work by the philosopher and psychologist John Dewey and political scientist Arthur Bentley, distinguishes three forms of communication: action, transaction and interaction (see Figure 3.1).

Figure 3.1   Action, transaction, interaction

ACTION

Communication as action is described as an 'act' involving independent 'actors' who 'activate' an event. In communication terms, this might be thought of as something that one person does to another, or 'getting someone's thoughts into another person's head', and it is decidedly one-way. It is the communication equivalent of an exasperated parent declaring, 'Because I said so.' If it has you bristling with disapproval, then it is worth reflecting that we are all capable of this. Our fantasy is that if only we can articulate our view clearly or powerfully enough, then others will buckle at our inescapable logic or potent rhetoric. We externalise the responsibility of understanding. In 2004 I was dispatched to Stockholm. The professional services section of the recently acquired Frango business was losing money, and Cognos's European Vice-President, David Ayling-Smith, and Operations Director, Alan Chapman, wanted a turnaround plan. There was initial and absolute resistance from the Frango management team when they believed that they where going to receive commands from the acquiring company. This quickly dissipated into co-operation in the absence of any mandates, and developed into complete collaboration when everyone realised that there would not be a single recommendation without a thorough understanding of their situation first. They turned their own business around within a quarter, and it continued to be profit-making long after my last flight home from Arlanda airport.

This externalisation of understanding is true of customer relationships, too. The first iteration of CRM in the 1980s can be characterised as 'database marketing' – the practice of building up large data sets of customers in order to target them with marketing messages. Database marketing is a lot of 'out' and very little 'in'. The Direct Marketing Association reports response rates as low as 1.38 per cent for letter-sized snail mail, and conversion rates of 1.73 percent for email. This means that businesses interrupt 98–9 people who are not interested, at least not at that moment, to talk to the one or two who are. We have built up an elaborate systems of junk mail folders, inbox rules, spam filters and telephone preference services just to reduce these interruptions to a manageable level.

Action-styled communication was and remains common inside the organisation. The sales manager who disciplines a sales representative for giving a customer discount rather than 'selling value' without taking time to review the account history would probably describe himself as 'prone to action' without understanding that while it is preferable to inaction, its effectiveness is limited. An example of this style of communication is referred to in *The Hidden Power of Social Networks*. The authors, Rob Cross and Andrew Parker, studied networks and their interactions in companies around the world. One interviewee articulated it this way:

> *Some people will give you their opinions without trying to either understand what your objective are or understand where you are coming from, or they will be very closed in their answer to you. But [she] is the sort of person that makes sure she understands what the issue is. I have been around people who give you a quick spiel because they think they are smart and that by throwing some framework or angle up they can quickly wow you and get out of the hard work of solving the problem. [She], for all her other responsibilities and stature in the firm, is not like that.*

TRANSACTION

Communication as transaction is described by Eadie as 'functional'. It takes the form of active inquiry at some stages, but held in reserve in others. It is an occasional exchange 'sufficiently equitable in the long run to keep most individuals in our society in the transactional relation'. If it sounds like the bare minimum, that's because it is. It describes a somewhat narrow, restricted relationship between businesses and their customers and their workers.

During the 1990s CRM became more transactional. Instead of just gathering data on their customers, businesses began to give something back. This was the golden age of frequent flyer, bonus points and other loyalty programmes as CRM became a two-way street.

Inside the organisation, transactional communication was common and preferable to action-based communication. Workers worked their 40 hours, and claimed 40 hours of pay in return. The need to be emotionally engaged was not consistently considered important. However, many organisations were beginning to reject a transactional relationship in favour of a more human relationship. These organisations unintentionally and informally formed a social contract with their staff. In return for working additional hours to meet deadlines and spikes in customer demand, staff took time out of work for childcare or other important commitments. Some progressive companies even assumed that their staff would take a small number of days off in addition to their holiday entitlement simply because they didn't have the energy or the will to work on the day. While increasingly rare in an efficiency-hungry process world, those firms that allow this refer to them as 'duvet days'. Transactional communication between the organisation and its staff and between the brand and its customers was prevalent, though. Conducted efficiently, it sometimes felt like interaction, but it rarely was. Customers knew this because they were delighted when business interacted rather than transacted with them, and despaired when the transactions failed. Recently, a colleague was stood in a long queue in the bank during his lunch break. Time was limited, but this was a transaction that could not be dealt with by any of the three machines in the banking hall, so he took his chances. Other customer transactions seemed to be being dealt with efficiently at the front of the queue until an exception occurred. The next customer had some form of non-standard enquiry, and the queue stopped moving and stayed that way for a full ten minutes. Transactions, even exceptions, were being dealt with, but the experience was not positive, and it was about to become less so. Another assistant was working his way through the queue making enquiries about the customers' provision for savings. The bank clearly wanted to take advantage of those rare occasions when a customer was actually on its premises. It wanted to ensure that those who perhaps only had a current account were aware of the competitive rates available to them if they purchased a savings product. As a transaction, assuming a well-managed queue, it made sense. It might even have been described in the management meeting where the idea originated as a win/win. However, any amount of interaction with customers at that moment would have concluded that this was a bad idea. Customers with limited time want to complete their business quickly. If, as will frequently happen, the speed at which the queue moves is slower than the time the customer has, they will become frustrated at the apparent diversion of resources away from dealing with the queue. Being informed about new products will seem trivial at best, and a naked sales ploy at worst.

INTERACTION

Information science describes interaction as 'reciprocal role-taking', 'the mutual performance of empathic behaviours'. The goal of interaction is the 'merger of self and other, a complete ability to anticipate, predict and behave with the joint needs of self and other'.

In the first part of the twenty-first century CRM began to introduce capabilities that supported a dialogue with customers. It was the first time the word 'relationship' in CRM was even being acknowledged. It was evolving to support ever more complex processes. However, interaction cannot be modelled on a customer service flowchart. There are too many arrows, decisions and exceptions. J. Jeff Kober, author of *The Wonderful World of Customer Service at Disney*, describes the problem with trying to build a process that delivers the legendary Disney customer service levels:

> *The typical tendency for leaders is to try and map out all the possible behaviours their employees should demonstrate when working with customers. This approach is flawed for two important reasons. First, such behaviours tend to come across as rote, rather then genuine. Second, it is impossible to map out all the potential behaviours individuals should demonstrate for future unforeseen circumstance.*

Kober was rejecting the process world wholesale because it didn't deliver what customers, or guests, had come to expect from one of the world best-loved brands: open, genuine, reciprocal and human exchange – interaction.

Investing in social media campaigns does not mean that a business is genuinely interacting with its customers, though. This is vividly illustrated in an IBM study, 'From Social Media to Social CRM', which identified that businesses mostly did not understand the real reasons why customers wanted to interact with businesses through social networks.

Businesses believed that the top two reasons consumers follow them in social networks were:

1.   to learn about new products (73 per cent);

2.   to receive general information (71 per cent).

However, the top two reasons consumers gave as to why they interacted with companies in social networks were:

1.   to receive discounts (61 per cent);

2.   to make purchases (55 per cent).

In fact, the top two reasons why businesses believed they were being followed were ranked bottom by their customers, and the top two ranked by customers were ranked bottom by businesses. The irony is inescapable. Those companies at the vanguard of customer interaction have not just misunderstood, but *completely* misunderstood the very reasons why their customers are interacting in the first place. We all have to start somewhere, though.

Misunderstanding is rife inside the organisation, too. A well-regarded Towers Perrin Global Workforce Study that we refer to in more detail later suggests that staff are either lukewarm or cool towards their employers. Management author Gary Hamel comments in his *Wall Street Journal* blog post titled 'Management's Dirty Little Secrets' that this is a 'stinging indictment of the legacy management practices found in most companies'. He goes on to suggest that there are only three possible reasons why managers don't respond to such evident failure on their part: ignorance, indifference or impotence. There are some managers who are interacting with their teams in meaningful dialogue. They are listening, participating and exploring ways in which to simultaneously build careers and create business value. They are simply not commonplace.

Management is Interaction

Business systems have not only left customers and staff cold in their loyalty to the process world, they have also left managers wanting. Managers essentially do four things: they plan, they monitor, they make decisions and they execute them. Decision making and decision implementation are poorly understood and even more poorly supported in the process world. Systems exist that support the planning process. Budgeting and forecasting can be heavily automated by performance management tools or lightly automated with spreadsheets. There are also systems that help managers monitor their business. A class of business systems that were first referred to as executive information or decision support systems have evolved into highly visual and interactive reporting and analysis referred to as business intelligence or analytics. Ask a chief information officer (CIO) how she supports her managers, and after an awkward silence she may concede that there isn't much beyond email, word processing, spreadsheets, telephones, meeting rooms and whiteboards, some of which the manager doesn't even plug in. There is an enormous systems gap. Managers, by definition, don't do things themselves. They get things done through others, they execute through other managers or through those who actually do the work – individual contributors. Getting things done through others is itself an interaction, requiring tools that organise groups. These tools exist, of course. In fact, managers probably use them at home to stay in touch with their family, friends, church and junior football club. They just haven't quite made their way inside their organisations, and if they have, their enterprise social platform has not found its way into their daily working practices – or at least not yet.

And all those processes will not stand still. Just when the business is enjoying a position of market leadership, a competitor or some previously unheard of insurgent comes along and disrupts the market. In an online world this can happen quickly. It might also surprise you, although I doubt it, that complex groups of processes don't always work as planned. Sometimes they are forgotten or they don't align with one another. Individual processes or groups of them can even break down completely. Even those that have become what the Six Sigma method refers to as 'black belts' have to deal with three failures out of every million activities. Process failure was probably behind the fact that my much-awaited Apple TV didn't work on Christmas Day 2010. Certainly, process failures were behind Toyota recalling 5.2 million cars in the same year because an accelerator pedal could get trapped in the floor mat. And they had more recalls to come. It wasn't a good time for Toyota, even though it has an incredible reputation for valuing its customers and its people and investing in processes.

Processes need to be managed, changed, improved and evolved, and fixed when they break. This is the world of decision making. It sits distinct to and separate from the process world in order for the processes to be observed and managed. While there is decision making inside the process world, it is operational. Operational decisions, right in the middle of a business process, need to be eliminated if possible, and if not, dealt with prescriptively by those who operate rather than own and manage the process. They need, wherever possible, to be a computation. If we place decision making on a continuum with 'calculation required' at the beginning and 'judgement required' at the end, then operational decisions would be somewhere to the far left of the line, whereas the process world needs it precisely above the 'c' in 'calculation required'. At its simplest level, decision making might itself be described as a process to identify a problem, gather a list of possible solutions and then select and implement the optimum one. However, on closer inspection it is a set of interactions. Decisions require the gathering of relevant information, analysis, debate, discourse and deliberation before finally reaching a conclusion and implementing whatever determination is made. And how do managers implement? By interaction.

Conclusion

Yves Morieux, a senior partner of Boston Consulting Group (BSG), explains in an article in the *Harvard Business Review* titled 'Smart Rules: Six Ways to Get People to Solve Problems Without You' that BSG has created an 'index of complicatedness'. It shows that across US and European companies, processes are undermining not improving corporate productivity. In fact, in the 20 per cent of organisations that are the most complicated, managers spend 40 per cent of their time writing reports and as much as 60 per cent of it co-ordinating meetings. That leaves little if any time for them to work with their teams or their customers. The reason is that over the past fifteen years there has been as much as a three and a half times increase in the procedures, vertical layers, interface structures, co-ordination bodies, and in the decision approvals needed in each of those businesses.

The same index is referred to in Lisa Bodell's book *Kill the Company*. Bodell, CEO of futurethink, describes how she has encountered companies so wedded to their procedures that they have allowed their processes to become their culture – efficient and accountable, but rigid and inflexible.

The systems to support such processes have been equally unyielding. They are, to a greater extent, transactional. Even those that might be considered people-centred, like HR and CRM, only deal with the essential operations. A whole career is captured in a handful of transactions – starting, leaving, promotions and annual appraisals. Customers, to whom every business is accountable, are captured as leads, contacts and opportunities. It is true that far more exchanges in the form of meetings and calls are captured in modern CRM, but it took us more than a decade to get even here.

Social tools, however, are engineered to facilitate and capture human interaction. These tools, have been widely adopted by individuals in their personal lives because they make organising effortless for families, friends, clubs, communities and other groups. They can help businesses for the very same reason. After all, a business is essentially a social group – just one organised for the purpose of creating economic value.

4

The Changing Nature of Data

Where is the life we have lost in living?
Where is the wisdom we have lost in knowledge?
Where is the knowledge we have lost in information?

T.S. Eliot, 'The Rock', 1934

SIGNPOSTS

- ✓ The real difference between data, information and knowledge
- ✓ The nature of 'Big Data'
- ✓ How new forms of data explain cause, and not just effect
- ✓ The opportunity created by a complete and authentic insight

---

The Age of Networked Data

In his 2011 book *Too Big to Know*, David Weinberger, co-author of *The Cluetrain Manifesto*, argues that the nature of knowledge is changing. It has, until recently, been shaped, even limited, by its old medium, paper. Now it is taking on properties of its new digital medium, the Internet. Weinberger, also the Senior Researcher for Harvard's Berkman Center for Internet and Society, describes the first two ages of knowledge as the Age of the Classic Fact and the Age of the Database Fact. Classic facts originated through meticulous research and were then committed to paper, pages, books and libraries. Database facts started with the introduction of 'data processing', which committed organisational facts to punched cards – pieces of stiff paper that contained digital data represented by the presence of holes. This was the point at which data and process became inseparable, the point at which business systems became, by definition, the sum of their data and the processing parts. As knowledge is shaped by its medium, systems are shaped by their data, and data by their systems. For example, the punched card could hold a single character on one of 80 columns. This limitation gave rise to many inventive shortcuts, including the practice of only storing the last two digits of the year because no one believed that these same systems would still be in use in 1999.

Historically, data in the form of discrete facts was constrained by the medium by which it was communicated – paper. This was also true of database facts at first. They were restricted by the number of characters on a card and the realistic limits of how many cards could be precariously stacked or stored. These restrictions disappeared quickly, though. Only a few short years ago, a terabyte was thought so unimaginably large that a corporation named itself and its database after it: Teradata. It was signalling that in the late 1980s, it alone could capture and process facts on the scale required by the largest of organisations. The terabyte is now a unit of home computing. During my first consulting assignment, the CIO pointed proudly at a picture on his office wall of their new hard drives being delivered. They were being lifted into the building by crane. Two drives, each a gigabyte in storage, a little on the small size for a camera now, had literally stopped the traffic. The database fact is now only constrained by the rapidly evolving nature of the digital medium on which it is stored – that is to say, practically limitless. In 1986 there were an estimated 2.6 billion gigabytes of analog data in the form of books, newspapers, vinyl, tape and film. By 2007, when we where all running out of libraries and shelves to store our 18 billion gigabytes of analog data, digital had overtaken, at a total of 276 billion gigabytes. As digital capacity continues to rise and costs fall, our capacity for storing and processing facts increases. Paper facts were scarce, digital facts are abundant, and becoming super-abundant.

Data, Information, Knowledge

Discussions of this nature with information professionals invariably turn to the difference between data and information, or between information and knowledge. These, sometimes heated, discussions are generally rooted in an understanding of a classification proposed by organisational theorist Russell Ackoff. Ackoff's classification of Data, Information, Knowledge and Wisdom (DIKW) came to prominence after he described it in his presidential address to the International Society for General Systems Research in 1989.

While Ackoff did not present the hierarchy graphically, it has subsequently been represented as a neat pyramid, to convey that information is derived from data, knowledge from information and wisdom from knowledge (see Figure 4.1). It was an evolution of a classification suggested by Harlan Cleveland in an article in *The Futurist*, where he referenced T.S. Eliot's 1934 work 'The Rock' – perhaps the original source of the DIKW pyramid. Of course, Eliot was not intending to make a contribution to the field of computer science, rather he was observing that in the non-stop hustle and bustle of living, we can lose something of life. He goes on to lament that in our unceasing desire for invention, we lose the wisdom in knowledge and the knowledge in information – all of which has never been more true. The evolving classification from Eliot to Harlan, Harlan to Ackoff was not an only attempt to characterise data, information and knowledge. Milan Zeleny, now Professor of Corporate Economics and Management and Economics at the Tomáš Baťa University in the Czech Republic, introduced a hierarchy in 1987 that started with 'know nothing', which developed 'know what', 'know how' and 'know why'. Others, including philosopher and Professor of Geography Yi-Fu Tuan and American sociologist and Harvard Professor Daniel Bell have also introduced classifications, none of which gained Ackoff's prominence. In short, Ackoff describes data as a product of observation, but absent of meaning. Information can be inferred from data, and can answer questions like 'Who?', 'What?', 'Where?' and 'When?', but only once we begin to link it together with relationships. Knowledge is know-how acquired through an understanding of patterns in information. Understanding is a cognitive process which synthesises new knowledge from the previously held knowledge. Finally, wisdom is an extrapolative process which might also be thought of as an understanding of the fundamental principles of knowledge. Speaking one language requires knowledge and understanding. However, speaking multiple languages teaches us something about the nature of language, which might be thought of as wisdom.

Data, Information, Insight for Organisational Decision Making

The challenge with Ackoff's pyramid is that it is trying to communicate too many principles: the difference between the state of unknown and known or unobserved and observed, the value that systems add to raw and unprocessed data, the cognitive leap from paper or screen to human understanding and the increases in human understanding, the pinnacle of which is characterised as wisdom. That's too much for one pyramid, chart or ladder.

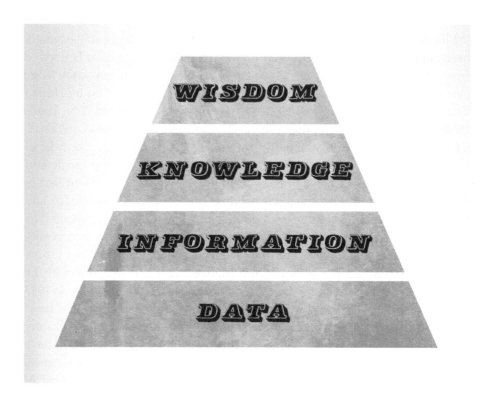

Figure 4.1   Ackoff's DIKW pyramid
Source: Adapted from Ackoff (1989)

In a criticism of the DIKW classification titled 'The Problem with the Data-Information-Knowledge-Wisdom Hierarchy', Weinberger argues that the term 'knowledge' has been hijacked. I agree. In an effort to distinguish ever-increasingly sophisticated technology solutions, practitioners replaced the term 'data management' with 'information management', then, when that didn't differentiate sufficiently, 'knowledge management'. We have yet to see 'wisdom management', but it is inevitable. We need to reclaim knowledge, to reduce information processing to a single step. This is not to diminish it, though. Technology advancements here have been remarkable, and there are many more to come. And while we might agree that this is somewhat of a semantic debate, it is important to distinguish between what machines do and what people do. What machines do is capture data and prepare it for human consumption. That's it – data to information. They do not 'know', at least not in the sense that humans do, and at least not for now. Anyone stood outside a London tube station staring intently at their smartphone deciding which direction to go next has experienced this. All the data are there, and they have even been organised into information in the form of visual cues – a map with street names, a compass, a locator pin for where you stand, and one for your destination. It takes a moment to understand what it all means, to synthesise all that information into knowledge, then action. The processing of raw data into information is what computers do. However, the journey from information to knowledge is a human one.

A simplification of Ackoff's pyramid is required in order to understand how human understanding is applied to organisational decision making. Many others have presented variations of Ackoff's pyramid, including economist Kenneth Boulding and American educator Nicholas L. Henry. Our own revision is a reduction, a simplification: the Data to Knowledge (D2K) Stack (see Figure 4.2). (Alternative acronyms were rejected for obvious reasons.)

The precursors to the first level are unknown data – data that have been unnoticed by the organisation are still data, they have just not yet been observed.

Which brings us to the first level in the stack: Data. Other DIKW revisionists have referred to data as 'observations', and this works well for the D2K Stack. Data are unprocessed, raw but observed in the very specific way that organisations observe. They capture data. They commit data to the organisational memory, a database or some other repository.

Information is prepared or processed from data, ascribing it sufficient meaning for it to be understood by a human. The D2K Stack is unconcerned with the degree of processing. It might, as Ackoff suggested, create relationships between the data, but this is a very narrow definition, rooted in a very specific technology: the relational database. This is also why technologists started claiming knowledge, because the steps from data to information and varieties of information are many. Information might take the form of tabular reports, charts and analyses, but it might be as simple as organised text. It is no coincidence that 'report' can also mean a document prepared as a result of a study, typically leading the reader through to conclusions from which decisions can be made. The D2K simplification addresses Weinberger's criticism. A single but sometimes giant step, from data to information, is intended to cover all processing, system or human, between raw captured facts and any document, report, chart or media from which a decision might be made. If, as Neil Raden, founder of Smart (enough) Systems advises, 'machines do the work and humans make the decisions' then machines must do the capturing, storing and processing of data into information whilst humans must ultimately do the understanding.

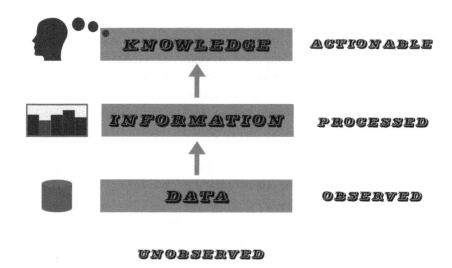

Figure 4.2   The simplified D2K Stack

The D2K Stack makes the cognitive leap from information to knowledge explicit. It declares that knowledge is not a product of consuming information. It is the result of a far more complex process involving the synthesis of information through a process of sense-making. It is also social, and in terms of organisational decisions, deeply so.

Transactional Data

In the nineteenth century a company would know or understand its own business through the pages of its journals, ledgers and books. These books were created by clerks who ordered raw facts into information in the form of leather-bound books. In Charles Dickens's *Martin Chuzzlewit*, the unscrupulous Tigg Montague exaggerated the longevity and dependability of his fraudulent insurance business, the Anglo-Bengali Disinterested Loan and Life Assurance

Company by pointing to the day-books, almanacs and green ledgers with red backs like 'strong cricket balls beaten flat'. Then, clerks would carefully maintain books for sales, purchases and cash in a way that remained fundamentally unchanged until the process was slowly replaced by computerised versions during the latter part of the twentieth century. Then organisations began to understand their business through facts captured, processed and reported as information by these systems in the form of 'computer reports' on what was called 'computer paper'. Computer paper was printed with so many columns and in such a small font that the paper had light green lines so that the reader could visually scan across accurately. For a decade or more these computer reports were bound in plastic folders using the same holes at both margins that had advanced it through noisy line printers. These folders did not bring to mind leathery cricket balls. Stacked high in a variety of primary colours, they were more like flattened Frisbees. Automated information did not need to look quite so impressive as the hand-crafted equivalent. The format of the printed information inside those inexpensive folders might have been the product of a number of systems evolutions, but still had strong reminiscences of the rows written carefully into leather-bound journals with a quill pen a century before.

The Age of Ambient Data

Today the process of capturing data is no longer limited by the number of book-keepers or to columns on punch cards. It has become not only possible, but practical and inexpensive for systems to capture every point at which they interact with their customers. A website can capture every click and action when we visit. It can analyse these clicks as if analysing us wandering around one of the company's stores, recording what we pick up to examine, what we put back down again, what we put in our basket but take out at the last minute just before we queue at the tills. It is not unusual for Web shopping sites to send an email if the electronic shopping basket was filled but abandoned. It is the electronic equivalent of the store manager sending a personalised letter as a result of your leaving your part-filled shopping trolley in an aisle because the queues were too long. In a process known as bi-variate or A/B testing, a business can maintain two complete and live versions of its website and analyse which is most successful at converting visitors to shoppers or which has the highest conversion rate. A more sophisticated version of this, multivariate testing, allows businesses to maintain multiple variations of their websites. Perhaps one uses simple product pictures, the other a more artistic set. Maybe one has secure payment assurances to the left of the 'Confirm Order' button, the other to the right, and a third places the assurances right next to the 'Add to Basket' button. An analysis of all the variations and the degree to which they encourage visitors to make an electronic purchase can help refine the website to the point where the customer has the best possible shopping experience and the business enjoys the maximum number of filled and paid-for shopping carts. Publishers who have magazines that can be accessed on tablet devices can measure the level of reader engagement with individual articles and advertisements as if the advertiser were sitting with the reader, with a stop-watch timing how long they stayed on the page.

It isn't just utility companies and smart meters that can generate billions of machine-to-machine (M2M) readings. We are able to do this for ourselves. The Knut (pronounced 'Canute') is a small battery-powered web-enabled, wireless sensor. The device monitors any environment, converting events into data. If a garage, front or fridge door opens or closes, the Knut will record it. If plant pots become too dry, basements too humid or aquariums too cool, then the Knut will make a note and send you a message.

Social tools allow us to share updates with no effort. In 140 characters or less, we can update a group of friends on what we saw at the cinema last night, the length of our flight delay or what we felt about the price of a cupcake as we queued in Starbucks. It's as if we can comment out loud in the queue at the box office, departure lounge or coffee shop and all our friends can hear. It doesn't matter if our friends are listening at that moment in time. We tweeted when we were held up in a queue, and they will consume the tweet as they wait for a meeting to start or during the commute home. This low level of continuous sharing has been described as 'ambient intimacy' by blogger and consultant Leisa Reichelt. Some consider it noise and irrelevance; others consider it positive and enriching – a way of maintaining a level of friendship across time and distance that would otherwise be impossible. Jeff Jarvis, author of *What Would Google Do?* and *Public Parts*, picked up the theme of ambient intimacy on his blog, BuzzMachine. Jarvis expounds that:

> *Ambient intimacy is about being able to keep in touch with people with a level of regularity and intimacy that you wouldn't usually have access to, because time and space conspire to make it impossible.*

Casual conversations used to be ephemeral. They were, as Rutger Hauer in the role of Roy Batty in *Blade Runner* poetically puts it, 'moments lost in time, like tears in rain'. Social tools now capture them for ever. Conversations between customers and other customers, between customers and the company and between workers inside the company are now captured as data, as persistently as transactions have been for decades. The data that organisations observe now include ambient data. Ambient data can now be processed to create new information that would have been impossible previously because of, as Jarvis puts it, time and space. Ambient data can provide valuable insights. If one person tweets about the price of cupcakes in Starbucks, it seems trivial. At best it tells you something about the tweeter. However, if lots of people tweet about the price of cupcakes in Starbucks, it can tell Starbucks or their competitors something about the price of cupcakes in Starbucks.

Ambient social data can help organisations find expertise that might otherwise remain hidden. Perhaps one of the young engineers in the San Francisco office was previously with a competitor or has skills that are not obvious from her job title or position in the organisation chart. This is data about people in our social group – in this case our social group being our company – that has only recently been shareable in this way. It might be that when joining a new team we discover that one of our new colleagues is part of an almost identical set of discussion groups, which provides an opportunity to build rapport and settle into the community more quickly. Enterprise social platforms can recommend new connections based on existing connections, tags, organisational relationships and the actions you have taken in other parts of the social platform. Like the professional social platform LinkedIn, they can illustrate the path that connects you to another person so that you can see the individuals who link you to a new and mutually productive relationship.

Clickstream, social and machine-to-machine signals are all ambient data. They are not limited to the conclusion of a set of interactions; they are the individual interactions themselves. Ambient data have always surrounded us – our gestures, conversations, the conversation we had with one another, our interactions when browsing or shopping in stores. Prior to the networked world, prior to ubiquitous computing and prior to the emergence of social platforms, they could only be recalled as anecdotes, as personal experiences. Now they are captured. They are observable facts. In the book *Competing on Analytics*, Thomas Davenport refers to one study of 450 executives in 371 companies which assessed the level at which organisations actively make decisions using analytics. One of his conclusions is that businesses should first establish a foundation of high-quality transactional data before managers can use systems for decision making. Today this is something of a limited view when the universe of observable data (see Figure 4.3) includes so many other

sources, such as text, video and social. In the near future this data will include
not just transactional but interactional data, too: ambient data.

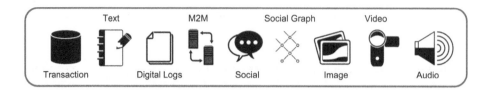

Figure 4.3   Extended universe of data sources

Characteristics of Ambient Data

Ambient data – a temperature reading, mouse click or a comment on a social
platform – are naturally occurring. While it might be a leap to ask you to regard
mouse clicks or tweets as natural, they are natural in the sense that they are
unprocessed – like natural cane sugar, if you will. They are representative of
their origins, and not artificially moulded by the system in which they have
been captured. If an employee has something to say about the new office, they
will say so not because they were asked, but because they felt motivated to
share their view with a colleague. They will not rate it against gradations of
'mostly satisfactory to mostly unsatisfactory', they will give it a 'yay' or 'boo'.
The data are not forced, solicited or limited by business rules, and they exist
regardless of whether the business observes them or not. They are pervasive,
ambient and diverse, and unlike any form of data business has used before.

Unlike transactional data, which is sparse, ambient data are abundant.
We are surrounded by observable ambient data, but until recently we have
not had the technology to capture them at a cost that we were prepared to
pay. Historically, classic facts were painstakingly gathered and captured, so
we had to be sure that they were of great value. They had to be fundamental,
universal truths. Likewise, database facts have previously been expensive to
capture and store, so we limited our attention to transactions. Today costs are
negligible. According to McKinsey in its report 'Big Data: The Next Frontier for
Innovation, Competition, and Productivity', the cost of storing all the music in
the world is $600, and falling.

As Table 4.1 shows, while transactions are carefully organised, ambient data have little or no structure. They can be a technical network log, any form of media, a microblog containing only loosely defined tags, a status update or an entire dialogue that barely follows the rules of natural language, let alone a sophisticated schema or layout.

Table 4.1   Characteristics of ambient versus transactional data

	Transactional	Ambient
Volume	Low to High	Super-/Hyper-abundant
Structure	Highly	Low or None
Individual value	High	Low
Rate of input/output	Low to High	Higher/Real-time
Value in aggregate	High	High
Individual precision	High	Low
Precision in aggregate	High	High

Classic facts were scrupulously edited before reaching the masses in books. Database facts have likewise been systematically but automatically validated to be definite and precise. They represent an invoice, a call centre support case, a dispatch note or a return. Each database fact is important in its own right. It is a record of an important event, the absence of which reduces the integrity of the organisational knowledge. Database facts are records of events generally accepted as significant by every business, so they are commonly understood, have a regular structure, are described in similar terms and have shared characteristics. If we summed up all the transactional facts in the world, theoretically, they should balance each other out; they should sum to zero. Conversely, ambient data are 'in the moment'. A single gesture can be accidental, a comment misinterpreted, and an opinion tweeted today can change tomorrow. It represents an idea, a speculation, an estimation and a notion. It is an emerging view, not necessarily a widely accepted one. There is nothing conclusive to be discovered in a single grain of ambient data, and everything to be understood from the whole. The treasure is in the aggregate.

Ambient Data: An Early Warning

Ambient data are different to transactional data in another important way. Ambient data are cause, transactions are effect. The transaction that records a customer closing their account may have followed a set of interactions with the customer service desk that were unsatisfactory. An increase in sales may follow a jump in the number of positive mentions of the brand. Ambient data are an indicator of future transactional data. In 2011, one hedge fund analysed conversations on social platforms between investors to predict price movements. Derwent Capital Markets employs software designed by Johan Bollen, Professor of Informatics and Computing at Indiana University, to understand sentiment and predict the direction of movement in the Dow Jones stock index. It takes a sample of all Twitter feeds and analyses sentiment and mood to determine not just whether the market is positive, neutral or negative, but also whether it is calm, alert, sure, vital or happy. It has proved to be an accurate predictor. In his study 'Twitter mood predicts the stock market', published in October 2010, Bollen predicted the movement of the Dow Jones in New York with almost 90 per cent accuracy.

Until relatively recently, business systems have been remarkably backward-looking. They have been a system of record providing an accurate insight into only that which has already happened, and have done a poor job of helping businesses understand why. In 1992 Dr Robert S. Kaplan and David Norton introduced an approach that was designed to change this. They observed that businesses focused almost entirely on financial information – the very final outcome of business activity. Companies aggregated all of those transactions and judged their success in terms of increases in revenue or decreases in costs. Kaplan and Norton believed that these measurements, by themselves, were insufficient. They tell us everything about past activity and nothing about the value that might be currently being created inside the company. Tomorrow's performance, they argued, is a result of developing innovative products, better customer relationships and motivated employees today. In fact, businesses could show good positive financial results in the short term by compromising the future. By not investing in training for the workforce, by alienating rather than investing in customer relationships, they could enjoy a significant, if brief, performance improvement. The approach of the balanced scorecard was adopted by many businesses across all sectors, including public and not-for-profits. The financial perspective was still important. It was the ultimate definition of organisational success, but it was accompanied by perspectives for understanding the customer, internal processes, and organisational learning and growth. The customer perspective articulated the unique set of benefits that the business offered its customers in the form of a value proposition. The internal perspective described how the organisation creates and delivers the value proposition. Finally, the learning and growth perspective describes how people, technology and culture supported and improved the processes. Kaplan and Norton later evolved the balanced scorecard into strategy maps. Strategy maps reinforced how value was created in the organisation through a chain of cause-and-effect activities that span the original balanced scorecard perspectives. Investing in organisational capability leads to efficient processes which deliver better products or services, satisfy customers and ultimately lead to good financial outcomes in the form of revenues and profit. For example, a systems integrator implements a training programme in project management (learning and growth). This leads to improved estimating (internal), and better estimates result in carefully managed customer expectations and increased customer satisfaction (customer). Ultimately, the financial outcome would be profitable projects and increased margins (financial).

Balanced scorecards and strategy maps are powerful conceptual models of how a business creates value through each and every activity. A business that understands customer, internal and learning perspectives can begin to understand their impact on financial outcomes. Measurement of innovation, employee capability, organisational learning and customer satisfaction are all leading indicators of performance. Financial indicators, including product revenues, are lagging indicators. Motivated and satisfied employees are a well-proven leading indicator of customer satisfaction.

Ambient social data are ahead of even leading indicators. If customers are voicing their dissatisfaction with a product and poor sales are unavoidable, then why wait for the next net promoter survey? If employee sentiment is increasingly negative, then why wait for statistics on staff attrition? Waiting for financial or other lagging outcomes is too late, but waiting for leading indicators is no longer soon enough. Staff have left, customers are making negative recommendations, and their interactions with others on social platforms are widely damaging now. Decisions to discontinue a product, reinstate training or address employee morale might reverse a negative trend, but the pattern could have been spotted earlier. A business interacting with its staff and its customers on social platforms will become aware of satisfaction or dissatisfaction as it happens, at the very beginning. Action can be taken as soon as the problem emerges.

The Big Finish

There is no superlative sufficient to describe the extent to which data are proliferating in the networked age. This can be the only logical reason why the technology industry has settled on the oddly inadequate term 'Big Data'. There are 30 billion items of content being shared on Facebook each month, half a billion tweets every day, 5 million trades per second and 350 billion smart meter readings each year. A million here, a billion there and pretty soon we are talking about serious amounts of data. In fact, 90 per cent of all the data in the world today has been created in the last two years. Google's Executive Chairman Eric Schmidt famously observed that between the birth of the world and 2003, 5 exabytes of information were created, but we now generate the same amount every two days. 'Big' doesn't really cover it.

It is not all about size either. Even the information management industry generally accepts that Big data has three characteristic - volume, velocity and variety in what has come to be known as the '3Vs' model. More recently a fourth v for veracity has been added to describe the imprecision inherent in a single item. Ambient or big data do not look like traditional data. Transactions, though not always well designed, are structured into columns and rows of a sort. Data from sensors, clickstreams and social sources are nothing like this, and nothing like each other. Social sources, even when processed, are streams of human conversation that make sense to the human eye but cannot be understood by traditional data processing systems. Instead, specialised platforms that can process natural language are required. We will cover these later.

While 'big' can be either relative or absolute, it does beg the question, 'How big?' The industry response to this is that 'big' is any volume of data that cannot be analysed using traditional processes or tools. Of course, this becomes somewhat problematic as 'Big Data' tools themselves become mainstream, so we propose an addendum to this definition: 'Big Data' describes the point at which it is possible to capture and analyse all that there is to know, all that is observable, all that is ambient.

For decades, systems have taken snapshots of business like a flip-book with all but the most significant pictures removed, leaving a jittery and fragmented record of activity. Organisations now have the capability to piece together a complete picture from every interaction between customer, staff and partners with their business. These are ambient data. Ambient data have always existed, have always surrounded, us but can now be heard, collected, understood and actioned.

5

Social Analytics

Not everything that can be counted counts, and not everything that counts can be counted.

Albert Einstein

SIGNPOSTS

- ✓ How businesses gain understanding through analytics
- ✓ A new class of analytics, new questions answered
- ✓ What a social graph is, and how business really gets done
- ✓ Influence and other newly measurable community dynamics
- ✓ The application of analytics as gamification

Understanding Through Analytics

Online retailers are, more than most, facing a time of technological change. They are continuously experimenting with initiatives like smart screens, in-store tablets and contact-less payment to stay ahead. One such business contacted us to help them with a problem that was less about technology and much more about understanding. Each year they were taking over $2 billion in orders but processing almost $1 billion in customer returns. The opportunity to reduce costs, or better still, almost double revenues was palpable. They just didn't understand the reasons for the returns sufficiently to reduce them. They were capturing the data, but the patterns were not obvious. They needed to understand the major themes behind why customers sent back which products under what circumstances.

Business intelligence and analytics help businesses make sense of the millions, even billions of rows of data from transactional systems. Reporting and exploring help to understand what is happening, while statistical analysis helps to identify the reasons why, through patterns in what might be millions, even billions of rows of data. In their book *Competing on Analytics*, Thomas H. Davenport and Jeanne G. Harris describe analytics as the 'extensive use of data, statistical and quantitative analysis, explanatory and predictive models, and fact-based management to drive decisions and actions'. One branch of analytics attempts to go beyond understanding the here and now to predicting future events from current data. Predictive analytics can identify those customers most likely to leave, and the purchase a customer is likely to make next. During customer interactions, predictive analytics can be used to recommend the best action from a list of possibilities in a marketing approach referred to as 'next best action'. They can be used to identify which parts are most cost-effective to replace during a routine car service and which businesses are likely to meet their credit obligations. The Italian football club AC Milan uses analytics to prevent player injuries. It uses a range of physiological, orthopaedic and mechanical data, much of it ambient, so that coaching staff can adjust training or introduce preventative exercises.

The emergence of social platforms and the capturing of ambient data are making new forms of information available, thought of as *social analytics*. The dominant forms today are marketing-related. They include customer reactions to products, brands and campaigns in the form of sentiment. The power of individual opinion, or influence, is another newly available measurement. Any analytic derived through social practices or from social sources is thought of as a social analytic. While the initial focus is outside the organisation, on customers, there is much to be discovered inside. Enterprise social analytics identify who is connected to whom, who has the expertise, those who are actively helping others, and who influences whom – in short, how work really gets done.

It's a Small World

There are many attractions at the Walt Disney theme parks that have proved to be enduring favourites with visitors, but none more so than 'It's a Small World'. The ride takes guests in a 15-seater boat around scenes representing the countries of the world populated by more than 300 cheery, waving animatronic children in national dress singing a song that visitors will never forget, even if they want to. It debuted in 1964 and should, by any rational analysis, have been eschewed by successive generations of increasingly sophisticated and consumer-savvy children. But it hasn't. It is so popular that the ride has been

replicated in Florida, Paris and even in the smallest of the parks in Hong
Kong. Even Disney 'magic' cannot fully explain its durability. Perhaps it is the
idea that we are all part of the same human family, that we are all connected,
that it is genuinely a small world that is behind its popularity. Hungarian
playwright Frigyes Karinthy enthralled his readers with this same notion in
his 1929 short story *Láncszemek* ('Chains'). One of Karinthy's characters bets
the rest of his group that they could name any person, and through at most
five acquaintances, one of which he knew personally, he could link to the
chosen one. To illustrate his point he links a Nobel Prize winner to himself.
He suggests that the Nobelist must know King Gustav, the Swedish monarch
who hands out the Nobel Prize, who in turn is a consummate tennis player
and plays occasionally with a tennis champion who happens to be a personal
friend. This idea – that it took six steps or fewer to connect any two people – was
taken from literary conceit to social experiment in 1967 by social psychologist,
Stanley Milgram. Milgram conducted a series of 'small world' experiments to
determine the average path length of a social network in the United States.
Milgram arranged for letters to be sent from either Omaha, Nebraska or
Wichita, Kansas to Boston, Massachusetts. The originators were instructed to
send the letter to a randomly chosen recipient in Boston or to someone who
was more likely to know them. A roster was kept for each connection so that
when the letters (actually parcels) were eventually returned to Harvard, they
could be analysed. A little over 60 out of the 300 letters arrived in Boston.
The average number of hops was between five and a half and six. At best,
though, this is inconclusive. Four-fifths of the letters did not reach the target at
all, let alone in six steps or less. The small world problem was too difficult to
solve with paper, but there was much more hope with digital equivalents. In
2008, researchers at Microsoft concluded that there are 6.6 degrees of separation
by analysing a database of 30 billion instant messaging conversations across the
globe. In 2011, Facebook's data team and the University of Milan analysed 69
billion connections and found that over 90 per cent of their users are connected
by only five hops or four degrees of separation.

   If Milgram was alive today he might have considered the extent to which the
small world problem can now be tested with a mixture of wonder and envy. No
letters, no postage – instead, connections are captured as ambient data. The effort
and energy required to perform a test constrained the original experiment to just
296 samples, while Microsoft and Facebook considered millions of individuals
and billions of connections across the world because they had the data.
Connections between individuals on social platforms are captured electronically,
making them available to interrogate, explore and analyse. Like all ambient data,

each grain is of little value, each connection tells us very little. An analysis of the aggregate, though, is of huge value. In this case it achieved what was previously unachievable: it solved the 'small world' problem.

The Social Graph, People and Connections

The data that represent this network of people and connections in a social network were referred to as the *social graph* by Mark Zuckerberg, CEO of Facebook, at its first annual conference, 'f8', in San Francisco in 2007. What Zuckerberg was communicating to investors, customers and the community of users was that Facebook had figured out exactly how its collection of ambient data, its social graph – an intangible asset – could create tangible value. This instantly popularised what was previously a term used almost exclusively by social scientists and mathematical theorists. The concepts of graph theory are easy enough to grasp. A graph consists of nodes and edges. A social graph is a mapping of people (nodes) and how they are related (edges). The digital equivalent is exactly what was required to solve the small world problem. Although Facebook has around one billion users, there is no single social graph whatever Zuckerber suggests. For example, many Facebook users will maintain their professional network using platforms such as BranchOut, Plaxo and LinkedIn. Companies that have implemented social tools inside their own organisation have their own enterprise social graph. And whilst Facebook has the dominant personal or 'lifestyle' social graph, there are many others such as Google+, Pinterest and Path. Some are specifically mobile and location aware (referred to as SoLoMo) such as Highlight and Banjo whilst others are for a specific community like Renren for Chinese speakers.

Analysis of a graph can expose a number of measurements that describe the node (person) relative to its position within the network. The simplest measurement, referred to as degree centrality, describes the number of edges or connections. It is a statistical analysis of neighbours. The connection or edge between each neighbour has direction. Graph theorists would say that it is 'directed'. When a fan of Ashton Kutcher follows him on Twitter, the fan has an outward connection, while Kutcher has another inward connection to add to the 13 million or so he already has. If we start counting degree centrality, then a person with a high volume of inward connections, *indegree* (Figure 5.1), can be thought of as popular. Similarly someone with *outdegree*, a high volume of outward connections, might be thought of as highly sociable or gregarious (Figure 5.2). This assumes that those connection types, like 'friend' or 'follower', are of a positive nature.

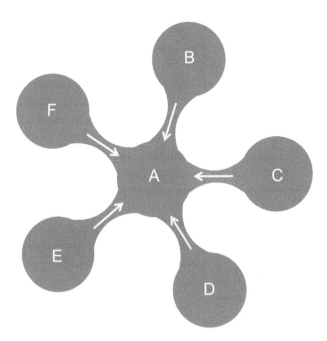

Figure 5.1   Indegree

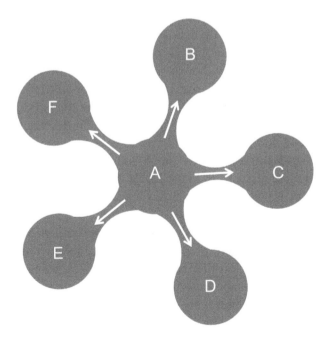

Figure 5.2   Outdegree

In an enterprise social graph, indegree is not necessarily an indication of popularity. There are many reasons for following others inside an organisation. The whole company will probably follow the CEO, regardless of the CEO's popularity. The CEO's status updates will be carefully chosen to reflect their leadership style. Jonathan Schwartz, CEO of Sun Microsystems, engages with his customers and his staff by communicating the company's successes and corporate wins. Jeff Bonforte, CEO of Xobni, believes that microblogging communicates the company's personality. Of course, those status updates might be about being stuck in an airport queue, in which case the CEO may find that they are neither popular nor widely followed.

An analysis of degree centrality can tell us much about individuals in an enterprise network. When looking at an enterprise social graph, those who stand out are those who have the highest levels of degree centrality, those who have the most connections. Instinctively, these feel like they are the most valuable, and sometimes this is true, but not always. In their book *The Hidden Power of Social Networks*, Rob Cross and Andrew Parker identify two types of highly connected people: the 'unsung hero' and the 'bottleneck'. The authors studied the informal networks of more than sixty companies. Almost universally, they found that certain people surprised managers by being more central than anyone would have anticipated. These people tended to engage selflessly in problem-solving, providing information and putting people in contact with others. Unsung heroes, by definition, usually go unnoticed, yet have a profoundly positive impact on the business. Their efforts to help others might consume hours every day, but they can go completely unrecognised by senior managers. Identifying unsung heroes can provide an opportunity for managers to acknowledge and reward them. While for many of these individuals being a good citizen is intrinsically rewarding, public acknowledgement provides further motivation and encourages collaborative and co-operative behaviours in others. Progressive companies could adapt their performance review process to include metrics from the social graph and reward unsung heroes, recognising them as heroes.

The other type of highly connected person is the bottleneck. A bottleneck may have engineered a central position in the provision of information or execution of activities in order to secure personal advantage and power. Managers need to fix this, because the bottleneck's self-interest is impeding others in the organisation. Not every bottleneck is jockeying for position. Many are well-meaning and are being overwhelmed. Others are in a role that has grown too large for a single person. Senior managers frequently find themselves in this position, and the bottleneck can be relieved by letting go and delegating some decisions to others.

Lifestyle social graphs can be mined for popularity of people based on lifestyle connections such as 'friend', 'family' or 'dated'. Enterprise social graphs can be mined for professional connections like 'managed by', 'trained with', 'same team', 'shared project' or 'collaborated with'. People, connections, conversations, comments and forums are all captured for analysis to help the organisation to understand the people and the connections in order to help them find people more efficiently, including recommending which other colleagues you might know but are currently not connected to. LinkedIn does this with 'People You May Know' in your professional network. This can also be seen in Twitter. When examining a profile, the connections will have been analysed to provide an insight into who else in your network follows them. IBM Connections can recommend people to add to your network based on existing connections with the 'Do You Know' widget. It can also show you the social path, the list of people who link you to a target person, with its widget 'Who Connects Us'. Socialtext 360 looks beyond the usual criteria for building teams, decision making or assigning people to projects. It indicates how members of a group are related not just by their business interests, but their geography, technical skills and interests.

New Nodes

Facebook users have always had the ability to add content to the social graph through the first generic but ubiquitous social gesture. Facebook users add pictures, video, music and other content to their social graph whenever they 'like' them. All of these things are naturally social – people routinely express their preferences for movies, albums and tracks – and now they are captured as ambient data, being added to Facebook's social graph. This makes the interactions between people and content, as well as people and people, available for analysis.

One of the first uses of newly implemented enterprise social platforms is usually content-sharing. Workers share and collaborate on presentations, documents and spreadsheets, as well as on business intelligence dashboards. These social objects, pieces of content, become additional nodes and edges on the enterprise social graph. Analytics can then identify useful content, useful people, or even new content from people who previously delivered great content. In spite of the importance of expertise in organisations, locating it has historically been carried out manually, and been time-consuming and sometimes haphazard, relying on referrals and reputations that can sometimes be opaque. The enterprise social graph contains all the data required to make expertise discovery easy. For example, Newsgator analyses user profiles and their interactions with content to help identify the right people for the job in the organisation. It allows the company to assign weightings so that the company can decide whether it is skills profiles, microblogging, answering questions, past projects or the way their content was rated by others that determines the extent to which they are an expert.

One feature of the Google+ platform, 'Ripples', is a rich visualisation using analytics to show the chain of sharing that takes place when content is shared from person to person. For example, it is possible to see the ripples, the series of consequences caused by a single post in 2012 that linked to a spoof TED talk to trailer the Ridley Scott film *Prometheus*. Google is a consistent innovator in dealing with the huge volumes of data required to achieve this. In a single interactive visualisation, it is possible to see who shared the content, the timeline for which it has been shared, and that there have been over 1,085 instances of this post being publicly shared. It is possible to zoom into and see the detail of who is sharing within each circle. While far less visual, a feature in the IBM Connections enterprise social platform does the same thing. Downloads and recommendations for documents, spreadsheets and other content are traceable so that content can be identified as highly regarded or highly used. This same data can be used to identify useful documents that might otherwise languish on a hard drive unnoticed. Yammer uses leaderboards to identify members with the most posts, members who are most liked and members who are most replied to. This allows the organisation to separate out those who are most active on the social platform and those who are actually contributing because their conversations are generating replies and ratings.

Extending the Edges

In 2010, Facebook announced the *open graph*: any website could add the Facebook 'Like' button to any piece of content, and in 2011 Zuckerberg announced a new version of the open graph which allowed people to not just share that they had liked content, but that they had simply interacted with it. The volume of interaction with personal social tools was about to explode. Partners working with Facebook and open graph could provide automatic, frictionless gestures. Spotify can generate a 'listened to' action, Foodspotting a 'cooked' action and Netflix a 'watched' without a single click. These actions and other verbs, including 'read' an article or 'ran a trail', were added to the social lexicon, and at the same time, Zuckerberg had allowed Facebook's partners to create totally new verbs, new social activity, for some of which an online equivalent had yet to even be invented. While lifestyle social platforms were adding cooking, running and listening, enterprise social platforms were adding verbs that represented activity that goes on in the workplace. Some of the verbs were shared. Reading in a lifestyle social platform relates to articles and books; reading in an enterprise social platform relates to documents, reports and materials related to the activity of the business. Rating a document is also similar. In the workplace, though, it can be used to increase its relative importance, allowing it to be noticed and perhaps used by more people. Other enterprise social gestures are likely to be specific to the workplace. Yammer allows managers to praise, and Socialtext provides a gesture that allows co-workers to thank one another. Others, like Facebook's open graph, are frictionless. Files are marked as downloaded and read as they are read. As a content creator, it is not just rewarding to see who is recommending your content, but also who is interacting with it, through a method as frictionless as Facebook's open graph.

Community Analytics and Community Health

Almost all enterprise social platforms offer one set of analytics – those related to usage. The platforms are self-measuring: they capture and analyse ambient data about those interactions within the platform so that the organisation can assess whether it is getting a return on the time and capital it has invested in software. However, this is rather like buying an exercise bike and capturing how many times you use it to determine whether it was a good investment. We would generally measure how many times we use it to determine an improvement in our health rather than a good use of our wealth. Likewise, an increase in community membership might tell us something about the ease of use of the software, but it also tells us something about the community. After an initial surge of membership, a healthy community will continue to grow – even mature communities, albeit at a reduced rate. Another health indicator is: if members are taking part, are they contributing, what's the volume of content being added? There is a meme referred to as the '1 per cent rule'. Established by analysing early Internet network behaviours on platforms like YouTube and Wikipedia, it suggests that there is a low ratio of contributors to consumers.

The rule suggests that only 1 per cent will create content, another 9 per cent will edit, contribute or curate in some way, and the remaining 90 per cent will just consume. Understanding the ratio of contributors to consumers and benchmarking against, if nothing else, the 1 per cent rule will provide insight into the overall culture of sharing in the organisation. The community will be well served by identifying and encouraging contributors. Good content will attract and engage participants as well as participation. Analytics can be used to build leaderboards that identify the highest, most frequent, most liked or most highly recommended contributors and contributions.

Analytics on the social graph can also tell us how responsive the community is by analysing the time between a post and a reply. Timely responses in a community perpetuate new responses. Long delays cause activity to peter out. One enterprise social platform, Lithium, measures liveliness by analysing the frequency of posts and their distribution across the whole community.

Influence

As digital interactions flourish, there is an opportunity to understand how individuals sway the decisions of others. Lifestyle and professional social platforms are making the most progress here because customers have an unprecedented capability to communicate and affect one another with a potency greater than that of traditional marketing. As in the physical world, measuring social influence is nuanced, but unlike the physical world we have ambient data to work with. The quantity of Twitter followers, LinkedIn connections or Facebook friends is too crude an analytic. What's more, businesses are already 'gaming' this by buying Twitter followers in packs of 1,000 for £50 or less. Freely available reputation measurements systems like PeerIndex, Twentyfeet, Kred and Klout are providing deeper insight.[1] They provide metrics that help us to understand reputation and influence. One of the Twitter-specific tools, Twitalyzer,[2] delivers more than thirty metrics, including engagement, velocity and generosity. At one time, Klout measured 'True Reach', based on the volume of replies, references, retweets and other responses, as well as 'Network Impact', which measured whether an individual's connections have influence themselves. Klout simplified this system in 2012 instead focusing on the detail of each interaction, which it referred to as 'moments'. Kred allows individuals to add offline factors, too. It lets you add education, professional

---

1   http://www.peerindex.net; https://www.twentyfeet.com; http://klout.com.
2   http://twitalyzer.com.

achievements, honours and even frequent flyer points to supplement a digital with a physical reputation. Social influence is even being used as a proxy in the physical world. At a prestigious fashion event in Bal Harbour, Miami in 2011, the thick velvet rope of the VIP area was only unhooked for those with a Klout score of 40 or over. In 2011, Universal Pictures invited top influencers to advanced screenings of Matt Damon and Emily Blunt in *Adjustment Bureau*, and those influential in the field of design and technology found themselves at the wheel of an Audi A8 for an all-expenses-paid weekend test-drive courtesy of a programme called KloutPerks.

Intrinsic Motivation with Analytics: Gamification

Positive behaviours online need not wait for the annual appraisal to be recognised, they can be recognised as they happen with techniques that are derived from the world of gaming. Gamification platforms such as Bunchball, BigDoor and Badgeville use game design techniques and mechanics to engage members of enterprise social networks. Those who share links, post blogs or answer questions receive recognition in the form of points and badges. Kudos badges for IBM Connections that include 'Network Builder' for connecting to a minimum number of others, 'Awesome Answers' for providing answers to questions and a 'Thank You' badge which is awarded each time the engine detects that you have been thanked on your board, the enterprise equivalent of the Facebook wall.

Gamification is not new – companies have employed game mechanics to drive customer and loyalty programmes for decades. However, the use of game mechanics inside the organisation is a new application, and is being driven by the availability of social analytics. For the first time companies have a reliable, digital approach to 'keeping score'. The IT analyst firm Gartner predicts that very large Global 2000 companies will be early adopters of gamification, and that it will be adopted my most mid-size to large organisations by 2021.

The Trouble with the Enterprise Social Graph

Like the lifestyle social graph, the enterprise social graph is fragmented. Our physical professional networks extend beyond our own corporate buildings, not least into the offices of our customers. But we also work with partners on joint value propositions, with suppliers who are critical to our own products, and with many other advisers and associates. These organisations may not be using the same professional social tool as us; indeed, they may not be using social tools at all. Physical conversations started within one group inside the company frequently involve others outside the company, so the digital equivalent needs to do so as well. Some professional social tools permit this, as long as all contributors are using the same platform. Others share common interfaces that allow developers to add or share social features across applications and tools. One such public specification is Open Social. The original implementation was supported by Google, Plaxo and Salesforce, among many others, and was joined by others, including LinkedIn and Jive, as professional social tools gained adoption.

Conclusion

New and useful information can be derived from the addition of ambient social data. In lifestyle social tools, these analytics indicate popularity and influence. In enterprise social tools, they indicate who is really helping work get done inside the organisation, who is a bottleneck, and who else we might connect to in order to be more effective in the workplace. Once we add content to a social graph, we gain an enhanced set of analytics, indicating not just how well connected people are, but what they are contributing to the network and how useful their contribution is. Positive social behaviours that were once hidden from view are made visible so that they can be called out and even rewarded. A helicopter view of an enterprise social graph helps us to understand the level of activity so that we can understand how lively, how healthy, how vibrant a business community is.

One early innovator in social analytics, UK-based Trampoline Systems, helps businesses to build their enterprise social graph in order to manage expertise and identify relationship gaps internally and between them and their customers. Trampoline Systems's network analysis platform has also helped larger organisations to understand the risks when restructuring or how well their integration efforts are progressing after a merger or acquisition. The addition and integration of social sources into the portfolio of organisational data are significant. There is much we can find out from a node and an edge.

6

Networked Decision Making

Just as knowledge is becoming a property of the network, leadership is becoming a property less of the leader than of the group that is being led.

David Weinberger, Too Big to Know blog

SIGNPOSTS

- ✓ The end of the hierarchy as a one-size-fits-all decision framework
- ✓ The relationship between knowledge, decisions and organisation
- ✓ How management as a discipline has been corrupted
- ✓ How the enterprise social graph replaces the organisation chart
- ✓ New roles for inclusive decision making

Reorganisation: The Long Corporate Lever

In 2006, the CEO and Chairman of Yahoo! at the time, Terry Semel, presided over what would prove to be just one of a series of reorganisations. Semel dismantled the existing structures, centred on products, and replaced them with ones focused on customer segments. Semel described the changes as 'moving aggressively to deliver the most possible value to our key customers – audiences, advertisers and publishers'. In 2008, Sue Decker, to whom Semel had handed responsibility, made a number of changes to the structure, including a regional group focused on the United States. Then in 2009, Decker's replacement, Carol Bartz, announced another restructuring, including a unified products group. This was by no means the final reorganisation. In 2012, at the time of writing, Yahoo! announced Marissa Mayer, long-time Google executive, as new CEO resulting in further and significant reorganisation. All of this reshuffling was done in the name of better decision making. Semel expected the changes to 'speed decision making'. Decker was quoted as saying: 'The changes we are making today will help deliver superior global products for users and enable faster and better decision making.' Bartz blogged that the new structure 'will make Yahoo! a lot faster on its feet'. She also wrote that the company had gotten rid of its 'notorious silos' and could now 'make speedier decisions'.

CEOs tend to believe that structure has a significant – perhaps even the most significant – impact on organisational decision making, and therefore success. In their book *Decide and Deliver*, Marcia Blenko, Michael C. Mankins and Paul Rogers point out that nearly half of all CEOs reorganise their companies within the first two years. Most, however, fail – each a flawed attempt at decision equilibrium. In a study of major reorganisations, Blenko, Organisational Practice Lead for Bain & Company, discovered that less than one third delivered significant performance improvements. Businesses that want to improve local decisions flip to a geographical structure. Those that are innovating switch to a product structure, and businesses looking for closer customer relationships organise around their customer segments. Each structure creates its own set of points in the hierarchy where decisions are made: decision points of accountability and responsibility. Changing the hierarchy changes the shape of the points and the emphasis of the business. At the risk of some light stereotyping, a pattern dominated by finance might make the business more fiscally cautious, one dominated by engineering might make it more innovative, and on dominated by sales might make it more deal-focused. If there are too many decision points, the decisions take too long; not enough, and they may not be made at all. If you arrange the patterns in the wrong shape, decisions will not align with the strategic direction of the organisation. Like a sound engineer working with a mixing board, the CEO hopes to turn some levels up and some down to create the perfect decision making sound for every song the business might perform. This corporate game of musical chairs consumes vast amounts of resources, promises much, attracts headlines in the business media, yet mostly fails. When the music stops and the inner-most layer of wrapping paper is torn off, there is little or nothing inside.

The reason for such frequent failure is not the reorganisation, but rather the nature of organisational structure itself. Replacing one chart with another doesn't work, or at least doesn't have the impact that everyone hoped for, because very little has fundamentally changed. Semel wanted to move from product focus to customer focus, so he changed the chart. Bartz wanted the organisation to be faster on its feet, so she changed the chart. And the experience at Yahoo! is the rule rather than the exception.

As a business grows, the hierarchy tends towards functional specialisation. Staff then develop deep functional expertise, but at the expense of breadth, which relies on process. Where problems or opportunities cross functional boundaries, they are more difficult to resolve. Over time, each department effectively becomes a silo, so cross-functional expertise can only be applied to a decision if a layer or multiple layers of management are involved. If a CEO wants to shift focus, she changes these layers. She changes the chart. But changing the chart has stopped working.

THE BEGINNING AND THE END OF THE ORGANISATION CHART

The organisational chart has given us great service for a century and a half, but it simply wasn't built for businesses in the information age, it was built to solve a very specific set of problems in the industrial age.

One of the earliest charts, possibly the first in the United States, goes all the way back to 1855. Daniel McCallum, a Scottish-born engineer, wanted to solve the difficulties of managing larger railroads compared to smaller ones. The rapid growth of the railroad had created a conundrum. Small railways were making money, large ones were not. As General Superintendent of the Erie Railroad, McCallum decided that the problem was one of management. He observed: 'A superintendent of a road fifty miles in length can give its business his professional attention and may be constantly on the line engaged in direction of its details; each person is personally known to him, and all questions in relation to its business are at once presented and acted upon; and any system however imperfect may under such circumstances prove comparatively successful.' McCallum continued: 'five hundred miles in length a very different state exists. Any system which might be applicable to the business and extent of a short road would be found entirely inadequate to the wants of a long one.' His solution was to break up the railroad, by geography, into more manageable size. Each was headed by a superintendent responsible for the operations within his division, Each divisional superintendent was required to submit detailed reports to central headquarters, where McCallum co-ordinated and gave general direction to the operations of the separate divisions. Lines of authority between each superintendent and his subordinates and between each superintendent and headquarters were clearly laid out. In sketching these lines of authority on paper, the first organisation chart was published. Soon the other railroads copied the Erie's system, enabling the big railroads to function almost as effectively as the smaller ones, and enabling further, albeit not untroubled, growth. At the time, rail shares accounted for half of all securities traded in the United States, so railroads were synonymous with big business. If the organisation chart worked for railroads, it worked for business.

Nowadays, the organisation chart is omnipresent to the point where we barely question it. As an organisation grows in size, it typically begins to organise itself around a hierarchy. This can be functional (Marketing, Sales, Finance), grouped around a product or service, or as is common in the financial services sector, around a specific customer category. Barclays, whose divisions include Retail Banking and Corporate, is an example of this. Geography may also play a part, so that regional structures can manage across locations and international boundaries. Decisions are made by layers of management at each level of the hierarchy – decision nodes. A senior management team, answerable to the board of directors and shareholders, sits at the top of the pyramid. One or more levels of middle managers with functional, customer, divisional or geographical departmental responsibility are responsible to this senior management team. Finally, supervisory managers oversee the day-to-day operations of the level of staff who are the individual contributors.

However, the limitations of this system are obvious with even the most superficial examination. It has one dimension. Count 'em. One. The hierarchy. A single set of lines and boxes flowing vertically to communicate reporting lines, seniority, knowledge, authority and decision making responsibilities. This century and a half-old model assumes that your line manager is more senior, co-ordinates your work, is more experienced and more knowledgeable, and has more decision making authority than you do. While this may have been true 150 years ago, it is rarely the case today.

The Golden Rule: Whoever Owns the Gold

In classical economics, the factors of production are land, labour and capital. Some economists suggest that there is a fourth factor, enterprise or entrepreneurship, although this can also be regarded as a specialist form of labour. Place these three elements in a social group, and we have a business. Factors of production go in, products and services come out. There has been a pecking order to factors of production. In the eighteenth and nineteenth centuries capital was scarce while labour was abundant. The purpose of the hierarchy in serving the ongoing viability of the enterprise was then principally to make optimum use of capital. Without capital and continued access to it, there could be no business. When our economies were chiefly agriculture, landowners made decisions and farm labourers followed them. When economies were chiefly manufacturing, those who owned the factories made the decisions, and those who operated the machines obeyed them.

Capital continues to be crucial in creating new businesses. Entrepreneurs have an idea for a business, but need capital. Investors have capital, but need ideas. Some ideas will ultimately work, some will not. In order to fund the ones that will not, investors take a large degree of ownership in those that do. This is rational enough. Eric Ries, author of *The Lean Startup*, describes a start-up as 'a human institution designed to create something new under conditions of extreme uncertainty'. Uncertainty has a price. In order for markets to function, those who take the risk must see the reward, otherwise the market will not attract new investors, new risk-takers and new capital. The more capital-intensive the business, the greater the importance of capital, the more the owners of capital retain control and attract rewards. Capital also means that businesses can grow. Larger businesses mean economies of scale and a greater ability to compete on price and innovation. In highly commoditised markets, only those who deliver at the best possible price survive. Capital is as relevant today as it ever was. However, in twenty-first-century economics, while still vital, it is no longer sovereign; land and labour are no longer its subjects.

Knowledge Capitalists and Lean Start-ups

The need for professional, creative, skilled workers in order for a business to succeed has been slowly but inexorably increasing in importance to a point where the need for highly skilled labour is as great or greater than the need for capital. A round of funding, a capital injection, is increasingly spent on people rather than premises or machinery. At the same time, in a networked economy, land is not always land. Instead, resources and raw materials are increasingly digital. Even physical products rely on digital. Everything from a cup of coffee to a car at least partially depends on software, social, Web and apps. The resources to build these don't follow the same physical laws of scarcity. In fact, the time and cost of creating new digital products is falling dramatically as a result of ubiquitous access to a thriving 'commodity technology stack'. No digital business need start from scratch. Instead it has access to incredibly sophisticated but low-cost technology as well as free and open-source software.

Many digital start-ups are founding themselves at a fraction of the cost of not just their physical counterparts, but also their digital equivalents as little as five years ago. Eric Ries calls businesses that combine their use of commodity technology with an agile approach to business 'lean start-ups'. Land is no longer land, and it is questionable whether venture is venture. The most significant risk in starting a business, launching a new product or replacing an old one is that no one wants it. All that effort, all that time, all those resources may be wasted. What if a business could, before it committed resources to engineer, manufacture and ship a new product, guarantee sales of that product? What would the economics of a start-up venture be if this risk was eliminated? The answer is that it has been. Or at least it is starting to be. Commercial and social entrepreneurs can look to get their new product or project off the ground using the collective co-operation of a network in an approach referred to as 'crowdfunding'. If the crowd want it, they commit to buy it before it's made. New York-based Kickstarter is the largest social crowdfunding platform. Half of the team of 40 people manage the platform, and the other half manage the community of investors – or more accurately, 'pledgers'. Pledgers are not necessarily focused on economic reward. Their motivations vary, but because many projects are creative, they are often to do with being part of something rather than the accumulation of wealth. One of the most successful Kickstarter projects was a product called TikTok from designer Scott Wilson and his studio MINIMAL. In return for a pledge of $25, backers (pledgers) pre-ordered a strap that would convert an Apple iPod nano into a watch. Kickstarter operates an all-or-nothing funding model to improve the likelihood that its projects will succeed. TikTok set its target at $15,000. If it hadn't reached this amount or more, the project could not have gone ahead. However, by 16 December 2010 it had resoundingly left that goal in a rear-view mirror on which was written, 'Objects in this mirror may appear larger.' The project had raised $942,000 from 13,500 backers.

Those who pledge through crowdfunding platforms like Kickstarter and Wefund, Indiegogo and Sponsume receive imaginative perks such as personalised letters, autographed copies and backstage passes. A video game project, Roxia, offered to immortalise sponsors inside the game's virtual museum. There are more traditional benefits, too, such as access to the pre-released product or project. However, there is no equity sharing. The entrepreneur retains 100 per cent control. On the successful launch of TikTok and another range, Lunatick, Wilson didn't have to hand over a portion of his company to a risk-taking venture capitalist because there was no venture capitalist and there was little risk. Instead, customers voted for a product they wanted, and received it at a price that rewarded them for their pledge and Wilson for his innovation, rather than funding unsuccessful projects through the venture capital model. The crowdfunding model does not yet allow for equity sharing, although new legislation like the US Jumpstart Our Business Startups (JOBS) Act is an early attempt at balancing the level of agility required with the very real risk of individuals losing out to incompetent or fraudulent businesses. It is not a model that is set to undermine the NASDAQ or London Stock Exchange. Not just yet, anyway.

The dynamics between labour, land and capital have changed. Land is no longer physical, and economically, value is being created through knowledge, not just capital. The forces of labour are subverting the authority of capital. The impact of capital on a decision is not going to go away. Businesses don't survive if they don't have more capital coming in than is going out. This is also true for charities or not-for-profits. They carefully manage their capital by balancing donations with the cost of their charitable work. The public sector also has to work hard to control costs against a known and fixed income. All of this remains true: capital is an important factor. It is just not the only one. Those who own the capital don't have complete decision making authority any more, because capital is no longer the only wellspring of economic success. Knowledge, innovation, creativity, collaboration and agility are all sources, too. And they all need labour; they all need people.

Knowledge is Not Hierarchical

When the hierarchical structure served us well, the Head of Engineering was probably a former engineer. A shift manager in a factory was probably a former machinist, and a tailor was probably a tailor's hand five years previously. If an important decision was needed, the further up the hierarchy you went, the more knowledge and experience would go into the decision. Today, this is not true. The environment is changing too quickly. Ten years ago, Facebook didn't exist. By 2012, it had more than 850 million users and was on the radar of every marketing team. Five years ago, there was no iPad. In 2012 alone, over 100 million will be sold. A decade ago there were no such jobs as Community Manager, Search Engine Optimisation Specialist or Sustainability Manager, and there were no User Experience Managers. None. Today, managers may be managing individuals in roles of which they have no direct experience using tools and platforms that did not exist when they were moving into management. Community managers are managed by individuals who have seldom, if ever, been community managers themselves. Many software engineers have a manager who has never been a software engineer, at least not in terms of the current technologies. It is no longer safe to assume that knowledge and experience can automatically be found by searching up the hierarchy. Instead, they exist in an alternative network, undocumented by the single-dimension organisational chart.

This is why it is common in consultancy businesses to create communities of practice. A group of people outside the stated hierarchy interact frequently and over a sustained period to build up knowledge on markets, technologies, science and engineering. They lift the overall skills and knowledge of the entire organisation by overlaying a new chart over the hierarchy for this specific purpose. In fact, in many consulting businesses it is not uncommon to have your annual appraisal conducted by one individual, your career counselling by another, and the co-ordination of your current activity and your skills by yet another. It is still chiefly hierarchical, and incumbent management teams present traditional organisation charts, but a more accurate representation which also begins to demonstrate peer-to-peer relationships can be seen in Figure 6.1. This adaptation, like all bureaucracies, is not without its faults, but it is an indication that workers can cope with more complexity, more places to go for the things they need, if it makes sense. Rather than being confused or frustrated by this, consultants tend to take it in their stride. Of course, they tend to be naturally independent as a result of spending much of their working life working autonomously outside their own organisation, but it is not just this that makes it work. It is because they have figured out that in work, as in life, we don't get all things from one connection.

Management as Practice Over Progression

The organisation chart is also the way in which work gets organised. This is where we see the strongest correlation between the authority represented by capital and decision making through the determination of who does what. A single dimension implies that managers co-ordinate the work of others because a manager is one step closer to capital authority than the individual contributors they manage. If a team delivers revenue, the manager will be responsible for profitability. This will probably be called out on their LinkedIn profile as 'Profit and Loss (P&L) Manager'. If the team does not deliver revenue, then the profile will carry the slightly less prestigious, if not vaguely apologetic, skill of 'Cost Centre Manager'. They are managers not because they are skilled at

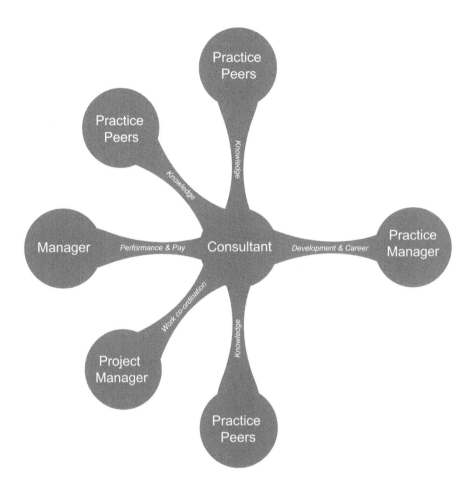

Figure 6.1   Practice management relationships graph

co-ordinating the work of others, but because they have been given stewardship of organisational economic well-being. The changing dynamic between capital and labour should mean that economic factors need to be an input into all decisions, just not the only ones.

The real challenge is that status and career advancement come from rising up this dimension. An accomplished engineer climbs the corporate ladder by becoming a manager of other engineers. A successful seller gains promotion through sales management. A skilled software engineer advances their career by becoming a project manager, then a programme manager, then a systems manager. In the interest of their career, individuals leave one discipline and enter another. They leave systems, sales or marketing, and become a manager of systems, sales or marketing. This form of career advancement assumes that those who are successful in their domain will be successful in managing others who are in the same domain. This does not necessarily follow.

Most have heard of The Peter Principle, the theory formulated by Dr Laurence J. Peter and Raymond Hull in their 1969 book *The Peter Principle*. The theory that employees are all eventually promoted beyond their level of ability is a common, if usually unfair, rationale for poor decisions. However, what is less well known is that the authors amusingly recommend a strategy of 'creative incompetence' for those who want to avoid the inevitable. Occasionally parking in the CEO's personal parking spot, for example, might cost someone a promotion, but not their job.

In fact, newly promoted managers often get off to a great start because they have an innate understanding of the work they have only recently stopped doing. However, the future may be shaped by the Peter Principle – not because they were not worthy of their promotion, but because their old skills will atrophy and their managements skills are new. Domain knowledge quickly goes out of date, so managers quickly shed the expertise of the people they manage. Meanwhile, their skills in organising people are emerging. Management is a skill and a discipline for its own sake. Erika Andersen, author of *Growing Great Employees* and *Being Strategic*, is emphatic on this subject. Commenting on the observation that one of the most common reasons that talented people leave organisations is poor management, Anderson recommends: 'create an organisation where those who manage others are hired for their ability to manage well, supported to get even better and held accountable and rewarded for doing so'. Henry Mintzberg, Cleghorn Professor of Management Studies at the Desautels Faculty of Management of McGill University in Montreal, asserts that management is not a profession, it is a practice.

If we decouple the co-ordination of the work from problematic notions of status and outdated principles of command and control, then the role becomes less about politics and more about making the right decisions. The role of the manager in networked decision making is either one of fiscal stewardship or organising for success, rather than posturing for power. Managers ensure that those who can contribute something to a decision are involved. Those who raised the issue, those who inform it, those who can offer feasible alternatives and those who are economically accountable all contribute to the common goal embodied in the scope and purpose of the decision. In short, managers manage.

Network Decision Roles

Organisational decisions are rarely made in isolation. I run the risk of stating what is obvious here in order to reinforce the point that organisational decisions are different to decisions we make as individuals for that very reason. They are decisions made by groups for groups. Understanding the roles individuals play in organisational decision making is complex. The single line in an organisation chart is inadequate, in the same way that some social platforms so satisfactorily distinguish relationship types. Paul Adams, a Facebook Product Manager and former social researcher at Google, led a study of social groups in the development of Google+ Social Circles and concluded that one-size-fits-all 'Friends' was simply unhelpful. We have family relationships, relationships with our colleagues and closer 'best' friends. We also have relationships that are built during life stages (such as university) or around hobbies (for instance, football teams, diving) and those that are built because of locality (for example, neighbours) As part of his research for creating Google+ Social Circles, Adams built up a picture of over 300 groups, 85 per cent of which did not even contain the word 'friend'. This is also true of the workplace. We have career stage relationships (fellow inductees) and neighbourhood relationships (same office), too. We might also have some that are temporary, perhaps based on projects and initiatives, and some that are more persistent and built around our function or domain (Sales, Marketing, Engineering). Roles also form around a decision. One worker may flag an exception, problem or opportunity, and is therefore the *originator*. That same individual may co-ordinate the activity involved in progressing the decision to a conclusion as a *facilitator*. The decision will require information typically provided by finance professionals or other *analysts* who have explicit knowledge to either frame the decision or inform alternatives. Others still will be *contributors*, either because they possess tacit knowledge, can provide ideas or their opinion is valued. Some will be *consulted*, perhaps because they will affected by the decision or because they will eventually be *implementers*, carrying out the decision once it is concluded. There may be others involved in formal *approver* processes, particularly in highly regulated industries, and finally, the *adjudicator* will make the final call. These decision roles are summarised in Table 6.1.

Table 6.1   Decision roles

Role	Description
Originator	Identifies the problem or opportunity and starts the framing process.
Facilitator	Co-ordinates the interactions of the other actors through the process of making the decision. Often, but not always, the originator.
Adjudicator	Has responsibility for making the call and will be accountable for it, often as a result of capital responsibility. Shared in a consensus, but not necessarily in collaborative decisions. If the group is formed by a committee, then the adjudicator will be the chair.
Analyst	Provides explicit information to help frame the decision or inform the alternatives.
Contributor	Trusted contributors provide tacit knowledge, opinion, creative input or contrary views with the sole purpose of improving decision quality.
Consultee	Consulted because they are affected by the decision. Implementers will typically be consultees.
Approver	Where formal approval is required. Executives with legal or regulatory compliance responsibility.
Implementer	Implements the decision. Inclusive decision making assumes that implementers are also consultees, so that decisions are arrived at with due regard to implementation.

In contrast to the eight decision roles, a hierarchy in its most basic form describes only one: that of 'reports to'. Figure 6.2 exposes how crudely the organisation chart represents reality. It does not shed light on how decisions are really made in an organisation, nor on how they can be improved. Figure 6.3 is a representation that is both richer and more rooted in reality.

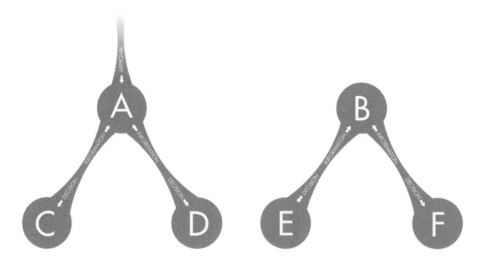

Figure 6.2   Hierarchical decision flow

Figure 6.3 Networked decision interaction

The standard organisation chart also poorly models decisions that overlap. Decisions made by groups often impact other groups. A decision to change the credit checking thresholds in the finance team will increase or decrease the universe of companies that the sales team can sell to. A decision by IT to replace an ageing customer service system because it is no longer supported impacts the customer services team which has to use it. A commercial decision to open for Sunday trading will impact everyone. In each decision, individuals fulfil one or more roles, with roles varying from one decision to the next. If each decision were a three-act play of alternatives, choices and actions, then the company would select a new cast for each performance.

As organisations rely more and more on informal, previously hidden networks, the formal organisation chart becomes increasingly irrelevant. Changing it doesn't work because it didn't represent how decisions were being made in the first place. The implementation of an enterprise social platform makes networked decisions practical. It also makes available and explicit what smart people in the organisation already knew – how stuff really gets done.

The Incompetent Hierarchy

In order for decisions to flow down from a decision node at which the judgement call is made, information and opinions about what is really happening in the business must flow up. Those higher up the pyramid cannot digest the volume of information that is being generated lower down, so information is summarised, distilled and stripped of detail before being communicated upwards. Nuance is lost because it needs to be. In summarising the meaning upwards there is a disconnect between the decision being made and the information being used to make it. There is a paradox here, in that the more important the decision, the less detail the decision maker will have on which to base that decision and the less time they will have to make it. One of the ways in which executives deal with this is to rely on information being provided for them. Kate Swann, former CEO of WHSmith has a reputation for insisting to her team that 'if they give her the data, she will give them a decision'. So senior decision makers will have a handle on a wide variety of factors that influence the decision, but each of the factors will be formally or informally summarised and simplified. In his startlingly prescient 1984 book *The IRG Solution*, David Andrews describes these and other limitations as 'hierarchical incompetence'.

We can see that sharing information up and down a hierarchy is problematic. By definition, the process of summarising information for a senior decision maker means a loss of detail. When problems are complex or nuanced, they are difficult to communicate, let alone summarise. But it is not just vertical communication that is problematic in hierarchies; lateral communication can also be hard. In some companies it can be stifled by departmental rivalry and the absence of an explicit network. What's more, in order for those at the top of the pyramid to scale, they tend to favour a small number of large solutions over a large number of smaller solutions, because they are easier to conceive and to manage. In the interest of economies of scale, small, local solutions are discounted in favour of sweeping changes. The inextricable link between hierarchy and status, according to Andrews, also drives behaviours that are about protecting status. Blame and praise are more important activities than those that fix mistakes or systematise success. Enlightened organisational cultures subvert the worst excesses of hierarchy, sometimes completely. However, hierarchy remains a symbol of outdated and rigid communication that is ready for the next evolution.

Trust Hierarchies: An Evolution in Networked Decision Making

In all of this, those calling the decision need a degree of trust from those who are involved in the decision making process. Today we talk about our 'trusted network', although we arrive at it through intuition and probably make no more than a mental note. Trust can be made explicit in online social networks. Members score, rank and indicate their trust of others in reputation systems that are integral to the network. eBay aggregates feedback from members so that the community has visibility of every other member's honesty, fairness and respect as a score. Epinions,[1] a shopping review site that shares its income with its reviewers, places great importance on unbiased reviews, making reviewer reputation and trust critical. It maintains categories including 'Top Reviewers', 'Advisors' and 'Category Leads'. It also encourages members to build up a 'web of trust'. By trusting another member, a reviewer is sharing some of their own social capital, their own trust, with them. Social platforms, using graph theory and analytics, can build up an accurate picture of trust. For example, in any system of reputation, the level of trust in an individual – what graph theory refers to as 'prestige' or 'deserve' – is not simply the aggregation of the level of trust from others. The calculation must account for the likelihood of each recommender to trust or mistrust others. The propensity of a node to trust or mistrust its neighbours – referred to as 'bias' – tells us something about the node itself. If a node is undiscerning and trusts all its neighbours, then its own trust should probably be weighted less highly.

What is currently being achieved in lifestyle social platforms can also be reflected in an enterprise social graph. The selection of individuals to consult when important decisions need to be made can be determined by their historical contributions to other decisions. Those whose input should be valued most highly should be based on the measurable level of trust gained in previous decisions. Decision quality can be improved simply by engaging those who have become trusted nodes in their network.

Conclusion

It offers some perspective if we recognise that the modern hierarchy was itself a replacement for another form of institution. The UK Poor Law Commission, founded in 1834, more than twenty years before McCallum drew his chart, was the model for most modern bureaucratic hierarchies. Prior to this, administrative

---

1   http://www.epinions.com.

and political offices were settled through a system of patronage. People such as Newton, who ran the Royal Mint, or Allen, who ran the Post Office, did so because they were friends or relatives of influential people. Landscaper Capability Brown, architect Wren and composer Handel were all appointed by a system of patronage operated by the informal networks of the aristocratic ruling classes. The growing middle classes replaced patronage with what they believed to be a system based on merit: the hierarchy. It was a radical, striking innovation, but is only a point in the evolution of organisation, not a destination.

Andrew McAfee of the MIT Center for Digital Business argues that organisations still practise decision making by what he calls HPPO – the Highest Paid Person's Opinion. However, social and economic change are slowly but irretrievably reducing the relevance of hierarchy. Reorganising to improve the quality of decisions is replacing one inadequate hierarchy with another. Success or failure are almost incidental to the new structure. This is because the hierarchy is a single dimension, trying to do too much. It is trying not just to communicate capital or economic responsibility – what we might call authority – but to communicate knowledge, skills, expertise, career development, decision making responsibilities and the co-ordination of work. It also infers the notions of status, trust and influence, all of which can be problematic and lead to cultural difficulties. Enterprise social platforms can separate the multiple dimensions, make them explicit, and expose new social graphs to help organisations understand and improve how information is shared, how work is done and how decisions are made.

In his book *Linked*, Albert-László Barabási describes how networks are pervasive in natural and human structures. They underpin the workings of the human brain, the Internet, social groups, even economies. They also closely model organisations, and yet we persist with a hierarchy. The network behind companies, like a 'tree', has the CEO occupying the root, with responsibility decaying down the branches. This structure, along with highly optimised, tightly integrated processes, leads to what Barabási refers to as 'a Byzantine monolith' – businesses so over-organised that they are completely inflexible and unable to respond to changes in the business environment. The hierarchy is suited to mass production, which was the way of economic success. Now, in the post-industrial era, economic success is rooted in agility, ideas and information. Now, companies face an unprecedented need to be flexible, and the hierarchy, like transactional attitudes, is no longer good enough. The organisation chart is already a falsehood, an idealised fabrication that provides no indication of how organisational decisions really get made. It has no place in the emerging social enterprise. It is dead. Long live the enterprise social graph!

7

Informed Decisions

What information consumes is rather obvious. It consumes the attention of its recipients. Hence a wealth of information creates a poverty of attention, and a need to allocate that attention efficiently among the overabundance of information sources that might consume it.
> *Herbert Alexander Simon, American social scientist and pioneer in artificial intelligence*

If you torture the data long enough, it will confess.
> *Ronald Coase*

SIGNPOSTS

- ✓ The importance of informed decisions
- ✓ How the origins of business intelligence are holding back its future
- ✓ Why the age of perfect information does not mean perfect decisions
- ✓ The indirect route from information to knowledge
- ✓ What is missing from decision support

Informed Decision Making

The need for decisions to be informed is self-evident. After all, the opposite of informed is unknowing, naive, ignorant, unwitting or clueless, none of which sound like robust strategies for arriving at the best possible outcome. Yet studies of organisational decisions consistently show that many decisions are made without making use of information at all. One study from the member-based advisory company the Corporate Executive Board (CEB), *Overcoming the Insight Deficit: Big Judgement in an Era of Big Data*, surveyed, 5,000 staff at 22 global companies and concluded that almost one in five decision makers seldom use analysis, and make decisions unilaterally. There is a clue to why this is such a significant subset in the author's decision to name this group 'Visceral Decision Makers'. Organisational decision makers don't describe the absence of information in decision making as uninformed. Rather, they describe it as experiential, instinctive or, to quote Jack Welch, 'straight from the gut'.

We know, though, that previous experiences can be unreliable, irrelevant and subject to bias. This can lead not only to poor decisions, but unfair decisions. For example, how should a lender make decisions about applications for loans and credit? Even in the aftermath of a global economic crisis, few would argue that a modern economy doesn't need an efficient market in personal financial credit. It has driven decades of personal freedom, social mobility and choice. It allows newly married couples to buy their own homes and graduates to buy a reliable car so that they can be at work on time. But how do lenders decide who does and who does not get approved? According to Larry Rosenberger, John Nash and Ann Graham, in their book *The Deciding Factor*, individuals like you and I would not have been able to get credit as recently as the 1920s. It was really only afforded to businessmen by other businessmen. The decision about who did and did not get credit was largely based on criteria that we would find objectionable today, including race and gender. It might also be based on highly subjective interpretations about an individual's honesty based on, for example, their punctuality. Then, social mores, opinion and prejudice determined an individual's access to potentially life changing lines of credit. Today, it is awarded based on employment status, income levels and credit history through scoring systems like FICO, the development of which is covered in Rosenberger, Nash and Graham's book. Over the last eighty years we have transformed a system of determining the financial future of individuals from one based on instinct and subjectivity, perhaps even unfairness, to one based on objectivity and on relevant, accurate and meaningful information.

Decision Making Systems

The decision about who gets their loan approved and who does not is just one decision – one that today is largely automated. Businesses make hundreds, thousands, even many thousands of decisions each and every day – who to hire, what level of discount to apply, which suppliers to partner with, which products to discontinue, which services to launch, which marketing campaigns to prolong, which have outlived their impact, and when and where to open a new retail outlet. These decisions are routinely informed with systems that provide insights into which retail sites deliver the most revenues per square foot, which suppliers offer the best prices, what discount levels stimulate sales volumes, and which products and customers deliver most or least profit. This information is diverse and contained in many separate operational systems, many of which provide good information in themselves, but none of which can provide a full and integrated picture. This is left to a set of systems and technologies that have come to be described as *business intelligence*. Business intelligence is a software category dominated by the major vendors SAP (Business Objects) Oracle (Oracle Business Intelligence, referred to as OBI) and IBM (Cognos), and the challengers to them like Tableau, Qliktech, Good Data, Panorama and many others which are absent from this list – an indication of shortage of space, and no indication of their market standing. These are individual tools that provide reports, analysis, alerts, dashboards and scorecards or comprehensive suites that comprise many or all of these functions.

Business intelligence is not just limited to understanding what has happened historically. Tools that deliver predictive analytics provide some indication of what might happen in the future. They manifestly do not include a crystal ball, but rather statistical and quantitative analysis of past events to calculate the likelihood of future ones. For example, many householders in the United Kingdom continue to purchase their telephone service through British Telecom and their domestic gas supply through British Gas. There is a category of customers who find something comforting in purchasing from a supplier whose name implies they provide to the nation in spite of the fact that these services were privatised in the 1980s. It is unlikely that British Gas or British Telecom are going to lose these customers any time soon, but businesses like these will almost certainly be calculating the chances of this happening each time these – in fact, all – customers interact with them. They will be able to predict the likelihood of each customer cancelling their service, or their 'propensity to churn'. Propensity to churn is a predictive analytic. Customers likely to churn might be offered discounts or new products, or they might be flagged as a high priority if they call into a customer service centre with a service issue, so that their call is dealt with quickly. Conversely, special promotions might be offered to customers with a lower propensity to churn. No one likes being overwhelmed with updates and special offers, so the approach to stable customer relationships might switch from awareness and promotion to lighter maintenance and nurturing. Propensity can be thought of as inclination or tendency – that is to say, it relates to a future behaviour rather than a historical one. This is what makes propensity to churn a predictive analytic. It provides an opportunity to spot future opportunities or problems, but to make decisions about them today. Predictive analytics are increasingly being introduced to the organisational decision making process. The likelihood of converting an occasional visitor into a regular shopper, that a credit card customer will default, that a transaction taking place right now is fraudulent and that two or more products might be purchased together in the same basket (affinity) are all predictive analytics.

Information Systems, Not Decision Making Systems

I invite you to take a look at the websites of the business intelligence vendors, and you will quickly understand the correlation between information and better decisions. At the time of writing, the home page of IBM Cognos promises 'smarter business decisions', Oracle BI 'accelerated decisions', SAP Business Objects 'immediate decisions' and Microsoft 'faster decision making'. The purpose of these systems is demonstrably about faster and smarter decisions, and I have no truck with this. Informed decisions are better decisions – that is to say, they are better than uninformed decisions. That is not the same as saying that the only thing that decision systems need to contribute to organisational decision making is more information. It is true that decisions require information; it is not necessarily true that increasing information will lead to increasingly better decisions. Decisions can be based on quite enough information already. Yet today's decision support systems are still largely being built to solve a problem of information scarcity, whereas it is abundant. The first generation of decision systems was designed around the paper-based reports they replaced. It simply went from paper to screen. The next generation moved everything from the desktop and onto the Web. Reports that didn't look that much different could now be viewed in a browser rather than with an installed Windows program. Some reports even carried the names of their ancient ancestors through several generations of redevelopment, creating an absurd situation where a modern Web-based report is named variations of 'P9751' or 'C4811' because of long-forgotten operating system filename length limits and legacy naming standards. Each time the decision system was upgraded using new technology, sophisticated exploration and analysis capabilities were partially used or ignored because they had no equivalent in the old systems. Those in the business couldn't articulate their requirements without referring to the old solution, and those in the IT project team couldn't get close enough to the business problem to provide genuine innovation. The result is that decision systems may look very different, but are rooted in the way decisions were made twenty years ago.

This is a common phenomenon in the digital world. Books on the early Kindle e-book reader had no page numbers. They didn't make sense. Select a larger font, and the 200-page book is now 300 pages, a smaller font and it's 100. Instead, Amazon invented location numbers, which made sense in the new medium, but created a problem for those who depended on the old medium for citations, for example. Later editions of Kindle devices and software included both page numbers and location numbers. The page numbers are a design device referred to as the *skeuomorph*, from the Greek words for 'tool' and 'form'. Skeuomorphs are not limited to digital design. The power of a car engine is still inexplicably described as a multiple of horses, and car wheels can look like they have spokes even though their purpose is purely aesthetic. However, skeuomorphs are commonly used in digital design. The pebble digital watch has an e-ink screen with an analogue face, the iPad calendar has the rich feel of a leather-bound ledger, the iPhone notepad the feel of a legal pad and the overriding metaphor of the PC is that of a desktop, incorporating folders and a trashcan. Some skeuomorphs outlive their familiarity. That large key on the right-hand side of your keyboard with an arrow heading down and then to the left is an 'enter' key. It's also known as the 'return' key. Its origins are in the typewriter, which used a moving carriage to shift the paper up and down and left and right. A keystroke would move the paper one character width to the left. When the typist reached the edge of the paper, a lever at the end of the carriage was used to push the carriage all the way back to the right – a carriage return. Later, electric typewriters replaced the lever with a carriage return key, which was ubiquitous on computer keyboards right up until the 1980s. Of course, the enter key remains, but it is still sometimes referred to as the 'return' key, and that arrow heading down and left is a visual cue which dates back to a large black roller sliding all the way to the right with a jolt, and then gently completing its cycle by shifting itself and the paper wrapped around it one line down.

This poses a dilemma for digital innovators. They have to decide whether a new technology should include cues from the old technology to maintain familiarity, or whether they should abandon old conventions, take advantage of the new paradigm and be completely unconstrained by the old. Some innovations are untroubled by the phenomenon because they are completely new. Twitter, for example, is difficult to describe using metaphors because it is a completely new form of communication. Indeed, 'tweetup' – a noun describing a meeting or other gathering organised by means of posts on the social networking service Twitter – made its way into the *Oxford English Dictionary* in 2009.

Business intelligence applications or systems that provide information for the purpose of organisational decisions make frequent use of skeuomorphs. The function that distributes reports electronically to many readers, with each reader only receiving the section relevant to their individual responsibilities, is described as 'bursting'. Bursting originally referred to the physical process of separating fanfold printer paper spewed out of industrial-sized printers into sections for each recipient by flicking the perforations that separate the sections. Only one report is developed, only one is run. However, store managers in Bradford, Bridgewater or Bristol all receive a unique and separate profit and loss summary. This is a practical metaphor. It had a place in the physical world, and has been commonly adopted in the digital world. However, there is a real risk in framing all digital solutions in relation to a long-forgotten analogue world.

A metaphor that severely restricts modern information provision is that of the 'report'. A report more generally refers to a document that communicates the findings of an investigation, experiment, analysis or inquiry. In the era of mainframe computing it describes the output, as distinct from the batch input and processing of early systems, where reports were printed on 132-column listing paper. In fact, the page was so wide that it was difficult for the reader to scan across all the columns while maintaining their attention on the correct row. To help with this, the paper was helpfully pre-printed with light green bars. Some early business intelligence reports misguidedly recreated these iconic green bars for laser printers and screen versions of the report. These reports were not interactive in any way. They were 'batch'. They were produced at the end of the day, week or month. Each report had a cost – a small one, but a cost nonetheless. A desk can also only take so much paper, so these reports were designed to be general, to answer a multitude of questions. Columns were squeezed in, just in case, so that the tortuous process of requesting a new report from the Systems Department didn't happen too often.

The report is increasingly irrelevant, yet it remains the unit of information delivery in an environment where it is increasingly likely that it is going to be consumed on a tablet or a smartphone rather than a desktop. By the time you read this book, IT analysts Gartner have predicted that almost a third of BI will be consumed on a mobile device. Modern BI is a field characterised by non-stop innovation. Vendors are adapting to new platforms, and many historical shortcomings, although perhaps not all, have been addressed long ago. Reports are customisable, multiple variations can be accessed through simple filters, sorts and formatting that mean that the IT department need only be involved in the brand-new information requirement.

However, the assumption is still that information flows one way: from reports, charts and dashboards into the head of a single decision maker as knowledge, as actionable insight without 'passing Go'. This isn't how information naturally flows through decisions. It is further degraded by the reliance on another metaphor commonly used in BI, that of 'publishing'. More accurately, the metaphor includes publishing and subscription. The implication is that one group, publishers, has produced something final and static for mass consumption, and that information will be consumed by another group, subscribers. Publishers publish, and subscribers read. A symptom of how poorly the publishing metaphor works is the ubiquitous use of Excel as a front end to business intelligence applications. Astonishingly, a business can invest tens, hundreds of thousands or even millions of dollars in building an application that assembles and delivers integrated, consistent and up-to-the-minute information, and then allow it to be manually manipulated with a desktop tool as a final step. It's the equivalent of a water company providing pure and filtered water to every household but stopping at the door, so that we end up carrying water around the house in buckets. The solution doesn't prevent all possible uses in our home, it is flexible and adaptable, but the absence of that final few feet of plumbing ignores any hygiene factors. BI professionals imagine that Excel is being used because it is a familiar user interface. However, the reality is that it is also being used to assemble information from multiple sources, to add information from external sources, to change existing information, perhaps even to add information that does not exist in corporate systems at all. In a business world of increasing accountability and compliance, it lacks auditability and introduces the risks associated with human error and misinterpretation. However, it is proof positive that a wealth of interaction, sharing and collaboration around the information is happening after it has been published. It is proof that much of today's business intelligence has been built to behave like Web 1.0.

The term 'Web 1.0' is a retronym, a type of neologism that describes a new concept to differentiate it from a previous form. In other words, the first version of the Web wasn't called 'Web 1.0' until everyone agreed there was a Web 2.0. There had to be a reasonable understanding of the concepts and behaviours that characterised and differentiated Web 1.0 from Web 2.0. 'Web 2.0' refers to an accumulation of changes that evolved into an Internet that was highly participative, that allowed users to interact with content, that promoted sharing and collaboration through blogs, wikis and social platforms. There was no upgrade event. There was no single development, feature or occurrence that resulted in the new version. Rather, it evolved from the previous platform. It was made possible by improvements in the technologies that underpin Web browsers and the servers that they connect to. Its growth was accelerated by new services like Facebook, LinkedIn, Path, Wikipedia, Twitter and FourSquare and by the rapid adoption of connected devices like the iPad and other tablets. Broadly speaking, Web 1.0 was about publishing, Web 2.0 is about interaction. Web 2.0 is social.

Like the distinction between Web 1.0 and Web 2.0, information for the purpose of decision making is rarely just published, consumed and acted upon in a single, serial cycle. It is the subject of a large number of interactions, many of which will not have been anticipated by the publisher. Information that answers one question will often raise more questions. Individuals synthesise the information, arrive at a hypothesis, and want to test it by embedding their hypothesis with the information as annotation or commentary. This invites more comments, more interaction. Decision makers might share information and their conclusions, and invite suggestions from their network about what is the best next action – the most appropriate solution to a problem or initiative to exploit an opportunity. If decision making is interactive, then it follows that decision making systems need to be equally so.

Sense-making

Even consuming a report, dashboard or chart is not really 'consuming' at all. Consumption assumes a linear, one-way process. In fact, reading a report is largely interactive. Mark Madsen CEO and Research Analyst of Third Nature, in a keynote address at the Data Warehousing Institute conference in Orlando in 2011, suggested that this process was *sense-making*. Sense-making is how we give meaning to everything that goes on around us, how we internalise external events, the actions of others and data. It is a broad and fascinating discipline studied by researchers and theorists in the field of organisational studies, information science and human–computer interaction. It is a philosophical, cognitive and sociological field, but our interest is in how sense-making relates to reading that report, or more specifically, how it relates to our simplified version of Ackoff's DIKW pyramid and understanding how information becomes insight – the bridge between the systems and processes that take data to information, and the leap from there to knowledge. In systems engineering terms, this last step is the bridging of the 'cognitive' gap' – the process of making sense of information. In his book *Dilemmas in the Study of Information*, Samuel D. Neill draws on the work of two very different theorists in the field of sense-making: Brenda Dervin, a professor at the Ohio State University School of Communications, and Karl Popper, who was a professor at the London School of Economics. Neill examines Dervin's argument that all information is subjective. This is an astonishing statement given that we naturally assume that 'the facts are the facts'. What Dervin argues, though, is that our capacity for information is both limited and selective. In a world of information abundance there is only so much we can process, so we discriminate each time we need information to make a decision. The process of seeking and using information is ultimately subjective. This means that knowledge is the sense made by individuals or a group at a point in time. It is only fact if is widely agreed upon. It can be disputed fact, controversial, or even just opinion if there is no shared sense of meaning or common agreement. Many academics note that sense-making is less about truth and more about plausible hypotheses.

Two other academics in this field, Peter Pirolli and Stuart Card published *The Sensemaking Process and Leverage Points for Analyst Technology* in 2005. It was a study into how intelligence analysts created new insights about political coups, bio-warfare threats and the behaviours of drug cartels from massive amounts of data. Pirolli and Card observed that the process was both bottom-up, where information was used to create theories, and top-down, where theories were tested by analysing information. The two major loops were foraging and sense-making. Foraging involved searching and filtering information, and sense-making involved the iterative development of a mental model or meaning. Both major loops were influenced by expert skill that enabled the analysts to skim and reject some information. The sense-making loop is about generating hypotheses and evidentiary reasoning (managing information to support or disconfirm hypotheses), all of which are subject to bias.

In organisational decision making forums – meetings – sense-making is a dominant activity. About one in three meetings that we participate in at work are to make decisions, and about a third of the time in these meetings is spent on reviewing the information, the reports and the dashboards, and agreeing what they mean. Take, for example, a problem involving a healthcare device manufacturing and supply company. During a regular monthly meeting a Senior Sales Director for their Surgical Devices division in Europe tabled an issue. He had spotted a dramatic decline in sales of disposable surgical scalpels. The problem had been identified by a group of information specialists and analysts based in the UK who routinely provided product-level sales reporting. However, the reason for the decline was unclear, and the meeting concluded without agreement about what the problem was, let alone what decision to make. The Sales Director, though, tasked his team with finding out more. His team did not just go back to the UK-based analyst for more information, it also started to ask questions of its networks. After a number of sellers had made calls to their closest and most trusted customers, they discovered the reason behind the fall in sales. The market had been flooded by inexpensive Chinese imports. However, before the business reacted to the competitive threat, more information came in from other sellers. Faulty packaging meant that high numbers of the Chinese-made disposable devices were not sterile, so were being rejected without being used. Customers were already planning to return to their old suppliers and abandon the cut-price equivalents. Information was critical in alerting the sales team to the problem. Information was also used to validate the price differentials and the scale of the problem and to inform the levels at which the business might need to discount. Ultimately, it was intelligence gathered by conversing with the firm's customers that allowed it to conclude that it actually needed to do nothing. Sales would soon revert to their normal levels as customers realised that they had been indulging in false economy.

The Scattering of Decision Artifacts

Meetings are toxic, according to Jason Fried and David Heinemeier Hansson, founders of 37signals and authors of *ReWork*, yet even the most progressive organisations see the need for properly run, short and efficient meetings – forums for making decisions, for example. They might take place as video or telephone conferences, they might even take place in virtual meeting rooms or as virtual conferences. Decision making meetings are typically monthly management meetings, quarterly business reviews, or in fast-moving businesses like retail, even daily meetings to make merchandising decisions that impact the day ahead. They are typically functional, and involve at least two layers of managers – for example, the Global SVP of marketing and her management team of perhaps regional VPs. In turn, the VP of say, Europe would hold equivalent meetings with country-level directors. These meetings are intended to keep the business on track, to measure progress throughout the year against a plan which has also been put together in similar meetings.

The format of these meetings varies wildly, but they will almost always include a review of the period that has just passed and an assessment of the latest forecast of the period ahead. The journey of the business is assessed from the perspective of what's just happened and what's about to happen. My experience of these meetings is that less time is spent decision making, and more is spent reviewing the information and agreeing what the information means. If there is any doubt about the accuracy of the information or disagreement that it is correct, then decisions will be deferred, their timeliness undermined. Unless there has been a collaborative effort prior to the meeting to establish a consensus on the current state of the business, then more time will be spent on this than on the process of making the judgement call and planning how it will be implemented.

Generally, one individual will have responsibility for summarising the meeting in minuted form, along with actions. The other attendees will also have been keeping notes in their daybook throughout, and once completed, they might transfer their actions from the minutes or personal daybook to their electronic task list. For those less organised, the meeting minutes will suffice. All follow-up will be conducted through email, meetings and phone calls. So let's recap. Critical decisions about how resources are going to be allocated will be discussed, and yet the artifacts of this critical decision making forum are scattered into documents, spreadsheets, emails and personal 'to do' lists. Tiny fragments of the discussion, information, conclusion, decisions and activities bounce around the organisation, never to be properly connected again except through the flawed recollections of a management team fatigued by the continuous need to recall the positions of previous decision making forums. Social decision making systems could associate information, decision artifacts and the actions taken as a result of the decision. Further, they could capture the success or failure of the decision, as well as the individuals that contributed to the decision. Over time, this would allow businesses to build up a picture of what decisions work under what circumstances, rather than relying on fallible human recollections.

Examples of the use of social tools in Chapter 8 illustrate how different collaborative decision making can be in the social enterprise.

The Physical/Digital Two-step

Digital solutions are designed to meet the needs of real-life problems. In turn, we work with digital solutions and arrive at new, efficient ways of working. Systems mimic the physical world, and life adapts to new systems in a continuous waltz of systems evolution. The music to which these two players dance is the unrelenting innovation fuelled by software companies competing to be first, best or both in their category. Systems and the problems they solve, though, can get out of step with one another. Take, for example, the idea of the 'start-of-day dashboard' in decision making systems. It's a commonly held prediction of a fully informed future where managers start their day by consulting a dashboard that will describe the status of their business in its entirety through gauges, charts and dials – a perfect picture in information. A variation of this sees a senior management team gathered around a boardroom table surrounded by screens providing moment-by-moment updates. The assumption is that every corner of the business can be described in data, every event, every twist and turn unambiguously interpreted so that the decision maker has a complete and accurate reading of the business through a cursory glance of visualisations that include spark, pie and bar charts. Exceptions or additional information can be explored by drilling down into more detail. The intense laser beam of information leaves no room for ambiguity or shades of grey. Instead, the empiricist manager can take fully informed, decisive and certain action without so much as making a phone call.

In reality, there are no managers who start their day in this way at the moment, and few who anticipate doing so any time soon. The reason is rooted in what really happens over that first cup of coffee. The first activity of the day for most is opening their inbox. It is as common as it is instinctive. The reason for this is that it reflects our commitments, often our unresolved commitments, to others. Email is the prevailing, if flawed, system of interaction. It is a record of interchanges that we pick up in the morning where we left off last night. It serves as a proxy 'to do' list. The threads of conversations are an indication of how the rest of day's, even the week's, priorities will unfold. This priority, this commitment to assess our interactions, is a reflection that our activities, including organisational decisions, are as determined by our interactions with others as they are by information.

Another unlikely scenario proposed by business intelligence idealists is one where senior managers react to a potential problem they have identified in their summary report or dashboard by exploring the data themselves. This is only considered plausible by those who don't actually interact with a management team. The primary resource available to most senior decision makers is not systems, but other people. A CEO made aware of a dip in revenue or a spike in costs will almost always consult with their management team first. A Global VP of Sales will look to their country managers rather than their scorecard for an understanding of why there is a variance to plan. Strategic problems or opportunities are illuminated in offices, corridors, on conference calls and email threads, not on computer screens. It is simply not the way a management team interacts with one another.

Conclusion

Decisions made on the basis of instinct and received wisdom show a vestigial reliance on past experiences which were relevant in the nineteenth and twentieth centuries, but are increasingly less so in twenty-first-century businesses operating in rapidly changing markets. What was true yesterday may not be true today, and is unlikely to stand up to tomorrow. Up-to-date information can replace entrenched and out-of-date views with fresh insights. This is not to dismiss the usefulness of experience. Visceral decisions can be made at speed, while purely empirical decisions require a diligent analysis of the facts each and every time. This is why most good decisions are made with a combination of information, experience and interaction.

Most business intelligence technologies have their origins in the 1980s. They were engineered and designed for a very different workplace. Telecommuting was rare then, while commonplace now. Today, workers in larger businesses collaborate with colleagues in different locations every day – in the 2009 Forrester study, *US Telecommuting Forecast and The Future of Work*, the proportions were almost 25 per cent daily and more than 70 per cent at least monthly. In the same study 87 per cent of knowledge workers said they spent time working with individuals outside their own organisation. These trends have continued to a point where the people we work with today are rarely in the same office, frequently not in the same company and commonly do not even share a time zone. The notion of getting together in an office around a published report to make decisions is becoming increasingly outdated.

Decision making systems, as sophisticated as they are in their dealing with information, fall well short when it comes to dealing with people. The same Forrester report revealed that those individuals involved in gathering information felt that their current systems did not help them gather information collaboratively, and that current communication methods – email and telephone – were time-consuming, error-prone and created needless additional work.

This widens the gap between decisions and decision systems. Information for the purpose of decision making is abundant. Its selection is a process that requires organisation and curation. Information does not leap off the screen into the collective organisational consciousness, rather it loops around in a process of sense-making that can involve many in establishing an agreed reality. What's more, today's decision systems don't capture the conversational threads, interpretations, determinations and actions that make up decision artifacts. These are left hanging and disconnected from the decision they support.

What is required is a not only an inclusive approach to organisational decision making, but a comprehensive framework of tools that support it, as Chapter 8 will reveal.

8

Decisions as Interactions

If you want to go fast, go alone. If you want to go far, go together.

African Proverb

SIGNPOSTS

✓   The myth of rational decisions and the reality of human bias
✓   How social interaction safeguards decisions
✓   What is missing from decision support systems today
✓   Where decision making tools sit in the social 4Cs framework
✓   The convergence of social and analytics for collaborative decision making

---

How Decisions are Really Made

On 15 January 2009, just 2 minutes and 32 seconds after US Airways Flight 1549 was cleared for takeoff from New York La Guardia Airport, Captain Chesley Sullenberger made a decision. A flock of Canada geese had disabled both engines of his Airbus A320 during takeoff, the aircraft was descending rapidly, and he decided to return to La Guardia immediately. Within 45 seconds, Sullenberger changed his decision. He changed his mind. Now less certain that he could make La Guardia, he spotted another runway, across the Hudson River at Teterboro airport, in northern New Jersey. At 3:29:03 he confirmed with air traffic control that he was going for it. Another 20 seconds later, Captain Sullenberger changed his decision one last time. As he was asked by air traffic control which runway at Teterboro, he replied: 'We're going to be in the Hudson.' The air traffic controller's request to 'say again' was never answered. At 3:33, 6 minutes after takeoff, evacuation began after the airliner, both engines critically damaged by bird strike, landed safely in the Hudson River. All 155 passengers survived.

The process that Captain Sullenberger employed that day is what Sydney Finkelstein, co-author of *Think Again*, calls 'one-plan-at-a-time decision making'. One-plan-at-a-time decision making is largely unconscious, intuitive and instinctive. It doesn't require discussion, debate, deliberation or even a conscious awareness that a decision is being made. It is a process of taking the first reasonable option, and selecting a new one if the old one doesn't work. One-plan-at-a-time decision making was critically successful on Flight 1549, when Captain Sullenberger was faced with a situation where the need for a quick decision outweighed the need for a considered one. It was a life-and-death situation. Inaction, or even delayed action, could have had fatal consequences.

The process is well designed to help us make quick or repeated decisions – those decisions that we make unconsciously every day where the call needs to be made in the moment. They are well suited to emergencies, to situations that require highly experienced individuals to decide quickly under pressure. Gary Klein, a cognitive psychologist, has spent more than twenty years studying just these forms of decisions. In just one study of 156 decisions made by firefighters, Klein found that options were considered only 18 times. On the other 138 occasions, firefighters arrived at one plan and executed it. These decisions rely on a wealth of experience. As Sullenberger said in an interview with news anchor Katie Couric:

> One way of looking at this might be that for 42 years, I've been making small, regular deposits in this bank of experience: education and training. And on January 15 the balance was sufficient so that I could make a very large withdrawal.

Organisational Decisions

There is a Swedish idiom, 'Det är ingen ko på isen,' which literally means 'There is no cow on the ice.' More fully, it is 'Det är ingen ko på isen så länge bakbenen står på land,' or 'There is no cow on the ice as long as the back legs are on land.' In other words, we are not in trouble. Not yet. Situations in which organisations need to make decisions are more often like this than they are the circumstances in which Captain Sullenberger found himself in on Flight 1549. They are not emergencies. There is time to make a considered and rational decision, to fully define the situation, identify solutions, consider them all, pick one, and implement it. In fact, most of us believe that organisational decisions are actually made in this way: the rational way. It is why we get so heated, as armchair critics, about the mistakes that organisations make. We ask 'How did Sony let Apple take the portable music player market?' or 'Why did Toyota end up recalling so many cars?', 'Why did smart people invest in Bernie Madoff?', 'Why did Boots, the second most trusted brand in the UK (Marks & Spencer being first), launch Wellbeing Services, and less than three years later, abandon them in the face of £100 million of losses when it was obvious that they were never going to work?' Of course, we have the benefit of hindsight and we are free from the responsibilities of making the decision ourselves. But we also assume that the original decisions followed a rational process, that in the absence of burning buildings or bird strike, these senior executives followed a full and rational decision making process. However, organisational decisions are more often made like Sullenberger's decision – one-plan-at-a-time. For more than a decade, Finkelstein has studied leadership and strategy from an unusual perspective. Rather than surveying best practice, his body of research is focused on worst practice – when things go wrong. According to Finkelstein, in almost all of the cases, a solid 8 out of 10, where he and his co-authors of *Think Again* had personal contact with primary decision makers, they appeared to have arrived at judgements without weighing the options. Their decision was made one-plan-at-a-time.

From the perspective of behavioural science, this is understandable. For most of the millions of years that our capacity for decision making has been evolving, indecision was the difference between eating or being eaten. Experience and instinct were the tools by which we lived or died. The other side of the 'coin of experience' is bias. For example, if we make a judgement too early, there is a large body of evidence that shows that we actively seek out confirming evidence and discount disconfirming evidence. We choose to synthesise some information into knowledge, and rationalise other information away. This confirmation bias is just one of the challenges. It turns out that instinctive, one-plan-at-a-time decision making is poorly designed to help us cope with ambiguous, complex or nuanced decisions. It doesn't help at all with new situations where we have little prior knowledge – in other words, important organisational decisions, decisions about merging teams, appointing new managers, acquiring other businesses, greenlighting projects, hiring new people. And organisations are growing more complex. In the 2010 IBM study, *Capitalizing on Complexity*, based on interviews with more than 1,500 CEOs, most believed they were operating in a world that is more volatile, highly uncertain and more complex than it has ever been before. And most believed there was more of the same ahead.

Social Safeguards

Finkelstein outlines four scenarios, four situations where human decision making is commonly flawed and should be 'red-flagged':

1.   misleading experience

2.   pre-judging

3.   inappropriate self-interest

4.   inappropriate attachment.

The most common misleading experience is a situation where the decision maker identifies strong similarities between a current and a recollected situation. Problems occur because of an over-reliance on experience while overlooking important differences. The mistake is in the nuance. According to Finkelstein, the sometimes disastrous results of red-flag decisions can be avoided by implementing four simple *safeguards*:

1.   Use experience, data and analysis.

2.   Create debate, and challenge.

3.   Practise governance to review the decisions.

4.   Monitoring performance, and adjust the strategy accordingly.

What's interesting about these safeguards is that they cannot be conducted by the decision maker in isolation. Debate, challenge and governance are activities that require communication with and inputs from others. Experience and analysis at their narrowest might take the form of information or hard data as an input into the decision making process. In their broader form, though, they are likely to require interaction, because we prefer to turn to other humans for information rather than computers. In summarising a decade of studies, MIT researcher Tom Allen, in his book *Managing the Flow of Technology*, makes this very point. Allen describes how he found that engineers and scientists – in other words, knowledge workers – were roughly five times more likely to turn to a person for information rather than an impersonal source like a database or a filing cabinet.

Even the hard data, while captured in a database, would most likely be conveyed by an accountant or analyst. People like learning from people.

Finkelstein's safeguards require increased levels of human interaction to keep decision making in check. The Stanford University Professional Certification Program in Strategic Decisions and Risk Management arrives at a similar conclusion. Highlighting the roles that multiple individuals in an organisation play in making a decision, Stanford insist that 'Decision Quality is brought about through structured interactions between the decision makers and decision staff.' It seems that making good decisions and averting poor ones require the same thing: interaction. Protecting the business from the cognitive bias and one-plan-at-at-time of the solo decision maker requires decisions to be more social.

Decision Support Gaps

In an increasingly complex world, executives are in need of systems support for strategic decisions. What used to be called 'executive information systems' or 'decision support systems' in the 1980s are now referred to as 'business intelligence' or 'analytics'. As the more recent naming of this field suggests, decision support has been largely limited to the provision of information. Barry Devlin, among the foremost authorities on this discipline, founder of 9sight Consulting and author of *Data Warehouse: From Architecture to Implementation*, describes the decision making process in what he calls the MEDA model. In the MEDA (Monitor, Evaluate, Decide, Act) model, Monitoring is about gathering the hard facts and what he refers to as 'soft' (what we would call 'ambient') information. This is Evaluated, summaries are built, analysis is carried out, and reports are drawn up and consumed. Then a Decision is reached through a collaborative process, and the decision is finally Acted upon. According to Devlin, and we would agree, BI tools to date spend all their time on the M and the E, and none of it on the D or the A.

That there is only fractional systems support can be seen in an example where my business had implemented such a system. A sales and stock analysis BI application for a health and beauty retailer revealed a poor historical purchasing decision that could only be corrected with timely and forward-looking action. At current sales volumes, the business had sufficient stock across all its stores for a full year's supply of a brand of condom with a short shelf life of only eight months. Visually, the problem was easy to spot because the analysis listed those products where stock levels were precariously low or inefficiently high. It was a category manager who made the connection to shelf life, as at the time it was not stored in data. This, along with solutions relating to pricing, promotions and shelf placement, were all discussed, debated, decided, implemented and tracked outside the BI application. This one, fairly typical and routine, management decision could have been better supported by an algorithm that joined up all the dots. However, as is commonplace, it was only partially supported by systems that were intended to deliver better, faster and smarter decisions.

Similar to Devlin's MEDA model, Figure 8.1 highlights three areas that lie outside traditional BI platforms. These decision support gaps, an extract of the Decision Source Framework for Organisational Decision Making, are:

• collaboration

• workflow

• monitoring.

These three gaps occur once there is collective understanding. The framework also identifies gaps in the cognitive process of getting from information to knowledge, as discussed in Chapter 7.

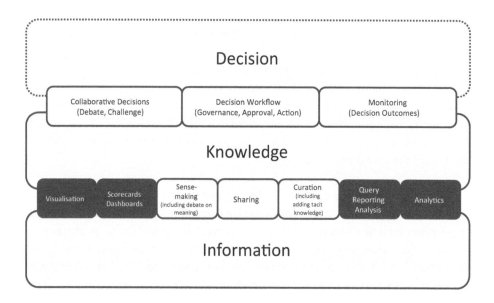

Figure 8.1   Decision support gaps

Decision Making and the Future of Work

The apparatus to implement social safeguards and to fill the gaps in decision support are to be found in the social, not the BI, portfolio. Business intelligence vendors have recognised this and started to add social. Some social vendors, for example Socialtext, approaching from the opposite direction have even begun to add BI. Others are filling the void by partnering and integrating: for example, Salesforce and Qliktech combining their Chatter and Qlikview tools. Microsoft and its 2012 acquisition of Yammer fit here too. Other mega-vendors, including IBM and SAP, with vast product sets including both social and BI, have already found ways to combine and package them together. Innovation from all the major software vendors is focused on filling decision support gaps with social.

Their customers, though, are not quite ready yet. According to Charlene Li's 2012 Altimeter report 'Making the Business Case for Enterprise Social Networks', companies that had deployed social tools didn't even consider decision making among their top five priorities. Instead, they wanted to improve collaboration, find experts or expertise, share best practices, evolve company culture and increase sharing. It would seem that the first job of enterprise social is to improve knowledge sharing. This priority is understandable given the importance of knowledge in many businesses. In fact, according to Peter F. Drucker in his book *Management Challenges for the 21st Century*, knowledge applied to tasks we know increases productivity, and knowledge applied to tasks that are new results in innovation. Knowledge is also, like a good man (or woman) in a Country and Western song, hard to find. According to the Butler Group, knowledge workers spend up to 30 per cent of their working day looking for data. In the network economy, knowledge is a rich source of value, and is tough to manage.

Tools for Enterprise 2.0 have thus far been mostly knowledge- or document-based. Tools like Microsoft Sharepoint have evolved the process of creating a document or spreadsheet from a solo act to a team activity. Fresh, innovative businesses like 37signals reinvented those activities that are naturally social such as project management and team selling, hitherto constrained by desktop tools, into wholly collaborative affairs with products like Basecamp and Campfire. Other tools, including wikis and blogs, have slowly eroded silos to make knowledge more available and accessible.

Collaborative decision making tools are nascent, they are the next major use of Enterprise 2.0 tools. Organisations are slowly waking up to the possibilities that automated social interaction benefits the highest-value organisational activity of all: decision making.

Niall Cook, in his definitive book *Enterprise 2.0: How Social Software Will Change the Future of Work*, presents a framework for categorising social software which he calls the '4Cs approach', reproduced and adapted in Figure 8.2. It helps us understand where business intelligence meets social

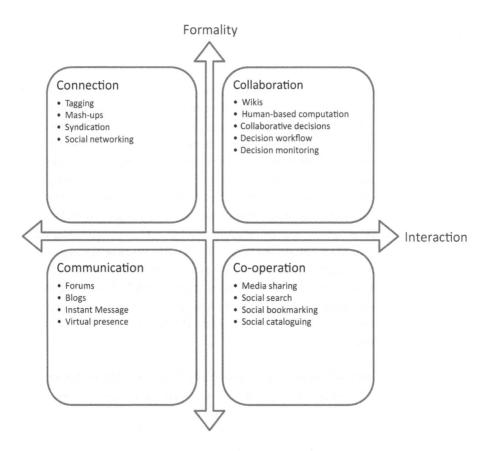

Figure 8.2   Enterprise 2.0, Niall Cook's 4Cs approach

Source: Niall Cook, *Enterprise 2.0: How Social Software Will Change the Future of Work*. Aldershot: Gower, 2008.

The framework characterises social tools as either for communication, co-operation, collaboration or connection. The 4Cs are distributed over quadrants built across two axes representing organisational culture: on the y axis formality, and on the x axis the level of interaction. For example, tools in the lower right quadrant for co-operation are informal but highly interactive. What is interesting is that the least densely populated quadrant is that on the upper right. Outside wikis, there is little else in this quadrant that is in common usage. This quadrant, formal but highly interactive, is the quadrant that is the most natural fit for collaborative decision making tools. Some of these tools, the decision support gaps they fill and their place in Cook's 4Cs framework are described in the following sections.

Informed Decisions and Social Safeguard No. 1

The first class of tool and social safeguard is all about ensuring that the decision is well informed, that there is insight into the problem and potential solutions. At first glance, this doesn't appear to be particularly social. This is at least partly because many systems providing this information have not historically been social by design. We have already seen this in the decision support gaps described earlier in this chapter. However, the platforms are beginning to make information more social. Scorecards, reports and dashboards are being combined with conversations. Sometimes the discourse questions the validity of the numbers or speculates what might be occurring in the business, and therefore what the numbers mean. This process, one of sense-making, is covered in more detail in Chapter 7.

In increasingly social business intelligence tools such as the *Qlikview Business Discovery Platform* we can see that information can be embedded in conversation, and conversation in information. The combination enriches the information and makes it more meaningful, delivering insight into the decision making process.

Debate, Challenge, Opinion and Social Safeguard No. 2

Networked decisions are, by definition, safeguarded because they are more social. Our rigid hierarchical organisation was limited here. As we saw in Chapter 6, the quality of a decision would be determined by the generalised nature of the latest reorganisation against the very specific requirements of the decision. In contrast, *networked decisions* enabled by enterprise social platforms quickly identify those individuals who can help in the debate and deliberation and allow them to form easily around the decisions in a group so easily formed it can be thought of as a 'pop-up'. Opinions can be gathered rapidly, while debate and discussion are unhindered by waiting for the next meeting or conference call. Those who might not have been conferred with because of limitations of time and logistics can now be consulted conveniently. Their views can be collected, and the resulting debate and discourse captured, understood and analysed. Established tools capture the conversations in groups and forums, but specifically for the purpose of decision making, placing them in Cook's upper right quadrant. In Figure 8.3 we can see an illustration which links the decision about renewing a contract with a convention centre with the geographical distribution of attendees, personal preferences, debate, opinions and requests for further information, all of which are typical when making a group decision.

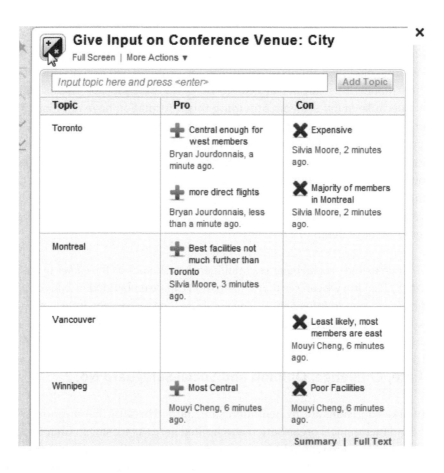

Figure 8.3   Streamworks Consensus Tools 1

Some platforms, such as SAP Streamworks, go above and beyond unstructured conversation. The platform includes a series of tools, including one intended to drive towards consensus by systematically exposing agreement and disagreement on an issue. The tool, illustrated in Figure 8.4, captures a statement, a stake in the ground, and in response to this statement, members of the team share their opinion in a column on a matrix that is either positive, negative or neutral. The tool is less about gaining consensus and more about capturing the mood of the team to stimulate some of the debate and challenge required in a good decision. Other tools allow contributors to be polled, to rank or to debate a well-framed decision statement.

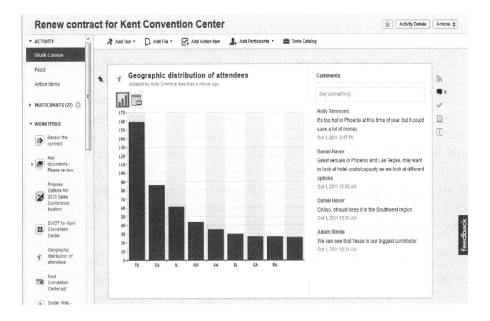

Figure 8.4   Streamworks Consensus Tools 2
© Copyright 2013 SAP AG. All rights reserved.

Creating a social tool for decision making does for decision making what it does for knowledge sharing. It reduces the constraints of time and space, it automates many of the interactions, it aggregates and records the decision for future analysis. At any one point in time, for example, previous decisions can be reviewed. Their outcome can be assessed in the light of new decisions so that future decisions can be improved.

Decision Workflow, Governance and Social Safeguard No. 3

Governance, like debate, is naturally social. An individual seeking approval is seeking the approbation of others. Those offering approval are granting permission to proceed to others, agreeing to an existing proposal, or acknowledging that it meets the requirements of the business. All are structured forms of interactions.

Of all the social safeguards, this is the most obvious to keep a decision in check and protect it from the risk of individual bias. Networks decisions, described in Chapter 6, more usually disperse decision activity throughout many roles. However, there may still be occasions when the individual who originated the decision is championing the preferred option and is also the decision maker – what we refer to as the adjudicator. Governance is a critical social safeguard here.

While approval can come from peer groups, teams, steering groups or committees, the default position for most organisational approvals is hierarchy. Traditional systems of approval, known as *groupware*, automate this type of governance, but their hierarchy and process-centricity can make them rigid, even brittle. This isn't to say that groupware isn't successful at what the organisations asks it to do, it's just that the organisation is still working through its hierarchy. More recent innovations, including ad hoc workflow, increase flexibility, but it remains top-down, explicitly assigning tasks according to competencies and roles, reducing senior managers, in many cases, to completing their part of a decision work flow just to keep their inbox down.

The ambition of social workflow tools such as Sparqlight, also in Cook's upper right quadrant, is to work like people do – to be more networked, less hierarchical. While groupware deals with transactions, orders, invoices, delivery notes or payments, social workflow can be wrapped around all forms of collaboration. It is able to embed discussions, information and other decision artifacts within the workflow so that reviewers and approvers can see all the data that the original decision maker could.

Complex decisions don't always respect hierarchy, and networked decisions (illustrated in Figure 6.3) are not limited by it. Decisions that require an approval use social workflow tools to invite participation based on the specific decision, not their position in the pyramid. While groupware tends to be top-down, social workflow can build in review points for those outside the hierarchy but within the network of influence as it relates to that decision. Fluid approval participation customised almost to a point of each individual decision enables a business to easily and quickly adapt to changes and deal with exceptions.

Monitoring Decision Outcomes and Social Safeguard No. 4

Monitoring the progress of a decision as it is executed is the last line of defence in flawed decision making, but is the first step in accountable decisions. Without monitoring, the actions taken as a result of the decision are often not systematically connected to it. In fact, according to one McKinsey study, 'How Companies Make Good Decisions', the outcome of 20 per cent of decisions were not even known. Twenty per cent of decisions, like Schrödinger's cat, were neither successful nor unsuccessful because once the decision was made, no one was sufficiently motivated to check inside the box.

Decisions that require significant investments of capital or time are often preceded by pilots or prototypes. This presents an opportunity to monitor the early stages of an implemented decision against pre-agreed success criteria, and can expose flawed or problematic decision outcomes. The most significant factors undermining effective decision monitoring are cultural. Reversing a decision can be perceived as failure, particularly for those who championed the decision. Planned check-points with everyone expecting and supporting a go or no-go decision go a long way towards minimising this.

Monitoring the implementation of a decision is little more than task management. In a meeting, conversation or through email a manager communicates what needs to be done, and the implementer, the individual contributor, records it in their 'to do' list. However, desktop task management is an island. A manager cannot monitor a delegated task without requesting frequent updates, or track progress without creating a duplicate. There are tools that help with sharing activity, that make up the upper right quadrant of Cook's 4Cs, including enterprise platforms such as IBM Connections, SAP Streamworks and Jive. These and others include shared activities so that teams can co-ordinate effectively. Figures 8.5 and 8.6 illustrate a scenario where a product category, Nova, has been declining in sales. Actions have been created to address the problem and increase sales by at least 10 per cent in the upcoming quarter. This situation, where information results in a decision, followed by remediation, all of which are coupled together in such a way that outcomes can be monitored, is incredibly powerful. It allows the business to monitor the quality of its decisions and build up a history of what activities work under what circumstances so that decision quality can be improved. Organisational experience is accumulated in the same way that individuals amass human experience.

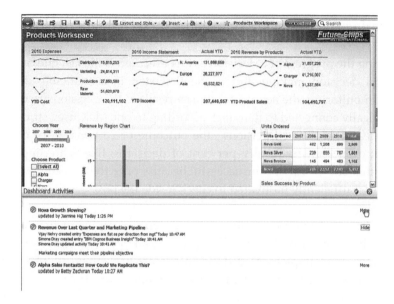

Figure 8.5   IBM Cognos and IBM Connections

Courtesy of International Business Machines Corporation, © International Business
Machines Corporation

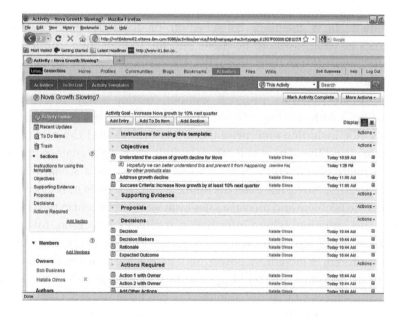

Figure 8.6   IBM Connections

Courtesy of International Business Machines Corporation, © International Business
Machines Corporation

Conclusion

Most organisational decisions are group decisions: interviewing a list of candidates and deciding on those who will go through for final interviews; deciding who is assigned to a new project; deciding whether a product issue can be fixed by allocating more staff to the problem or delaying the launch date. These decisions are littered with interaction. When decision makers want to surface differences, assess mood or get a handle on what the group feels is right, they go through what is usually an unstructured and conversational consensus gathering process. When a fixed list of options is available, pros and cons are weighed or the options are ranked in order of preference. All of these activities are group activities.

As humans, though, we are hard-wired for action. We do not always follow a rational process of decision making. Rather than evaluating a complete list of viable options, we rush to the first plan, and only change direction if it doesn't work. This can lead to heroic results for the individual expert in an emergency. In organisational decisions, not so much. Malcolm Gladwell points out in his noted work on intuitive thinking, *Blink*, that those intuitive short cuts that give us extraordinary powers of rapid cognition can also let us down. Human judgement is frequently skewed by an array of cognitive biases. Individuals can be over-optimistic, over-confident and subject to powerful but often unconscious attachment or self-interest. Research conducted by Sidney Finkelstein during the course of writing the books *Think Again* and *Why Smart Executives Fail* definitively establishes that most decisions that fail do so because the executive did not work through the options in any way that was meaningful.

Organisations provide an abundant resource to neutralise the cognitive bias in the solo decision maker: other people.

A social enterprise is one that has taken an approach and implemented tools that make inclusive decision making easy. Debate and challenge, monitoring and review are encouraged and supported. Decisions are not just safeguarded, they are optimised. Higher participation in decision making creates more decision alternatives, tests more hypothesis, considers more variables, weighs more pros and cons, and carries more contributors through the process in order that it can be implemented decisively. Organisational decisions in a social enterprise are more informed, more rigorously debated, more closely monitored. They are smarter and faster because they are social.

DECISION MAKING AND DECISION SUPPORT GAPS: EXAMPLE

Organisational decisions are only fractionally supported by today's decision support tools, which provide information but very little else. This is obvious if we consider a typical business problem, the points at which it receives system support and the points at which it does not, and we expose the decision support gaps described in Figure 8.1.

For example, the CEO of an engineering business spots a downward trend of its new electric car charger in Europe in marked contrast to growth to the US. The primary resource available to the CEO is other people. She does not analyse the problem further; instead, she asks her Chief Operating Office (COO) to investigate. Here we see the characteristic use of information in Figure 8.1, perhaps as a report, scorecard or decision. At this stage the CEO only suspects that there is an issue, and calls her executive team to action. Sharing and investigating in the form of sense-making is a gap.

The COO asks the VP of Sales and the VP of Marketing for help. Both have opinions on the reasons for the quarterly decline. The VP of Sales believes that this may be the recurrence of a problem with the company's distributor network, but the VP of Marketing believes that the recent appearance of a competitor is behind the sharp drop in sales in Europe. None of this is captured in traditional decision support. Both executives ask their teams for more information, and the co-ordination and connection with the original information are also gaps.

Their teams gather reports and insights into stock levels and competitive pricing, all supported. They also note that the product is considered superior in both European and US markets. They discover that the price differential is negligible; more then compensated for by the positive sentiment and perception of the product. Here, only stock and some pricing information are supported. Anecdotal, tacit knowledge and research commissioned by external agencies all sit outside decision support.

During a conference call later that week, the European Market Director overturns all previous hypotheses when she identifies the problem. Europe has, in the main, been growing, with the exception of France, which has not performed as expected. This she deduced from the data. All supported. However, she also knew that France had been focusing its advertising budgets on the major cities, including Paris, while the rest of Europe had carefully chosen commuter towns as being the richest sources of early adopters in electric motoring. After sharing her hypothesis with the local team and requesting the go-ahead from the VP of Marketing, she liaises with the French agency, changes the approach, and within a quarter sales begin to improve. From the moment she reached her epiphany on the cause of the problem to the point at which the European business turned around, she had no decision support.

Decisions need more than information. They need investigation of the root cause, they need to connect individuals with shared insight. They also need collaboration, work flow, and when the red button is pressed, they need monitoring for success or failure. Interactions safeguard against poor decisions, but are also the essence of organisational decisions. It's time for them to be supported, too.

9

Social Listening

Being heard is so close to being loved that for the average person, they are almost indistinguishable.

David Augsburger

SIGNPOSTS

- ✓ The power of listening, the most important social gesture
- ✓ Why social listening is more authentic than questioning and polling
- ✓ Listening with systems requires an understanding of human language
- ✓ Early examples of what we can learn through natural language processing

---

I'm Listening

A fan of *Frasier* right up until the last episode aired in 2004, I have often wondered what that closing song was all about. The song's composer, Bruce Miller, was asked to avoid explicit references to psychiatry, which explains the references to tossed salads and scrambled eggs. The second line, refers to the fact that Frasier might be a little woolly-headed, too, but this doesn't stop him from having the ability to listen, empathise and analyse others. In other words, confused he may well have been, but he still had them 'pegged'. Few would argue that the most important step in any form of communication – psychological, medical, commercial or personal – is listening. It is the subject of over 10,000 books on Amazon, with titles that include *Active Listening, Are You Really Listening?, The Wisdom of Listening* and *The Lost Art of Listening*. It is also the fourth of Dale Carnegie's Ways in Which to Win Friends and Influence People, and the fifth of Stephen Covey's '7 Habits of Highly Effective People'. Covey illustrated this point at one conference with a Native American Talking Stick. The Talking Stick was used when ancient council was called to allow each member to share their sacred point of view. If you had the stick, no one else could talk, and the stick wasn't relinquished until the holder felt understood. The approach is used successfully in many forms of counselling, using teddy bears, wooden spoons, even pencils. Its simplicity is that it ensures that everyone, as Covey puts it, seeks first to understand, then to be understood. The journey to becoming a social business can be summed up as moving from process to conversation, and while conversations with customers and with staff do require an authentic voice, they first require some authentic listening.

Businesses are swapping rigid processes for flexible conversations. In 2011, The Huffington Post listed the top 17 social companies, which included Apple, Best Buy, The Walt Disney Company, Amazon, Cisco and Google, In 2012, Fast Company listed the Top 25 social CIOs, which included mentions for SAP, Xerox, Home Depot and Dell. Social is not just for global technology companies, though. A Chicago cab driver, Rashid Temuri, chose to supplement the dispatch process with conversation. He offers what we all look for in a cab ride: a clean car, local knowledge and safe driving. If you want to take it further, though, you can follow him on Twitter as @ChicagoCabbie, and stay up to date with his check-ins and Instagram pictures of the city. You can book him directly without calling a central dispatcher, and opt for comfortable silence or healthy conversation.

Is a Process for Listening Really Listening?

Most businesses will claim that they have been listening all along. They have processes for it. They have surveys and polls. They can use customer surveys to understand how a new product should be priced or which logo is more popular, and employee surveys to determine how satisfied employees feel, and even how likely is it that they will look for a new job. These processes are time-consuming and expensive, so they are not continuous. Instead, they are snapshots, taken periodically or at key milestones. Also, not everyone is polled, and even if they were, we know that not everyone chooses to exercise their option to vote when given the opportunity to do so. This means that organisations are listening to a sample, rather than all their staff or customers. Feedback from a random, potentially unrepresentative or just plain vocal group might be highly inaccurate. Scientific polling attempts to deal with this. Scientific polls target a range of demographics – gender, age, race, income level, geography, religion, political affiliations – so that the results are representative and reflect the broader community. In spite of scientific practices, polling and surveying remain problematic. The primary objective of many people when being polled is to complete it quickly with relatively neutral responses. They are an imposition on our time, and they are not for our benefit. Offering small incentives doesn't really help, as most will want to get to the end of the poll quickly, unless they are particularly happy or particularly angry. Polls can also be created with the outcome in mind. It isn't very difficult to design a polling numbering system to support the statement, 'Most of our customers are either satisfied or very satisfied with our customer service desk,' while subverting the fact that nearly half were unsatisfied and some were even considering cancelling their service. No one wins from such an anaemic result – a box is checked, organisational culture remains unchanged, and customer service remains at a level where it is accepted, even if unhappily. These limitations are well understood and mitigated as much as possible, but mostly accepted, because businesses cannot obtain the information in any other practical way. At least not until now.

Social Listening

In contrast to polling, social listening is built on the premise that people are talking, in their own voices, in their own ways, in their own time, all the time. And they are doing so in their millions, compared to the typical poll sample of just a thousand. In 2012, IBM illustrated this point by analysing and scoring sentiment on Twitter around the World Series, Super Bowl and Hollywood awards. The results were interestingly and surprisingly accurate. On Saturday 25 February 2012, the day before the 84th Academy Awards, *The Artist* was generating the most buzz (7,693 tweets) and was in the top four for sentiment, along with *Midnight in Paris*, *The Help* and *Girl with the Dragon Tattoo*. *The Artist* went on to win the Best Picture award. It was a similar result for Best Actor, Jean Dujardin, whom I had the pleasure of meeting at the BFI London Critics' Circle Film Awards the previous month. He looked younger in colour. The prediction for Best Actress requires more interpretation. While Meryl Streep, who won the award, did generate the most buzz, there was stronger positive sentiment for all of the other ten nominees, and most for Charlize Theron in *Young Adult*. The predictions were unlikely to be perfect, though. They measured public sentiment in the millions, while there are actually fewer than 6,000 people who get to vote on the Academy Awards, one of whom is 101 years old and apparently not on Twitter yet. However, the thoughts of a few million people speaking freely produced surprisingly accurate results, and certainly more accurate than polling the views of a few hundred people willing to invest 20 minutes to answer someone else's questions on someone else's terms.

While these IBM illustrations were one-off exercises in predicting the outcomes of sporting and media events, Austin, Texas-based social consultancy the Dachis Group analyses signals from YouTube, Facebook, Twitter, Renren (Facebook in China) and many other social platforms in real time. Its approach is to measure not just brand sentiment, but also how effective organisations are being with their social engagement strategies. Their Social Business Index tracks the performance of global businesses in real time, has the look and feel of a stock market index, and uses similarly vast amounts of information in delivering it.

In 2012, to raise awareness of the Social Business Index, Dachis went head-to-head with traditional polling by taking on perhaps the most high-profile poll in the world. The Ad Meter poll was started in 1989 by the *USA Today* newspaper to determine the 'winning' commercial aired during the championship game of the American National Football League, the Super Bowl. The broadcast reaches 90 million viewers, and prices for advertising run to millions of dollars. The heavy price tag of the commercials has meant that the advertisers and brands are already the best-known and that the spots are reserved for first-time airings of their most innovative, humorous and sometimes controversial commercials. There are even large cash prizes awarded to the commercials' creators. Every year, the commercials are analysed live by *USA Today* in its Ad Meter poll with a focus group based in Virginia, the newspaper's headquarters, and one or more other sites around the country. In a nod to social media in 2012, Facebook and online *USA Today* users were polled in a second survey. That same year, Dachis published a detailed infographic comparing Ad Meter rankings with SBI rankings, along with other SBI metrics for brand awareness, love and mindshare. SBI and Ad Meter agreed on the outright winner, Doritos. However, Dachis believed it had a better handle on why. What its listening platform revealed was that Doritos garnered one million new video views, almost 30 per cent more subscriptions, and that the sentiment towards Doritos' advertisements overall was positive. There was disagreement, too. While Ad Meter ranked Coca-Cola at number 15, the SBI placed it second. The difference, Dachis explains, is that Ad Meter ranks each commercial separately, while the SBI picked up on the cumulative impact of three fairly traditional advertisements which connected with already large social communities, resulting in a further 700,000 subscribers to Coca-Cola's social accounts. This early and bold experiment in *social listening* demonstrated that there was a wealth of information on the impact of these million-dollar advertisements in the many millions of interactions and conversations that resulted from their airing.

Listening to the Workforce

The Super Bowl and Oscars are compelling and accessible examples of organisational stakeholders, in these cases customers, conversing about organisations, brands or products and waiting to be heard. They show how they have become organised and vocal through the use of social tools. The case for listening to customers is surely unquestionable. But those inside the firewall have become as vocal as those outside it. The workforce is as organised as the customers. After all, they are the same people. This was deeply concerning for the senior executives who attended a series of Social Business Briefings that we ran on behalf of IBM at the Royal Exchange, just a coin throw away from the Bank of England in the City of London. They were naturally troubled by the possibility that staff would air their grievances in public and affect their co-workers. 'How', they asked as the implications of social inside the enterprise dawned on them, 'will we control it?' Our advice was simple: 'You can't.' An enterprise social platform is not like its previous incarnation, the intranet, where the conversation was largely one-way. Instead, it will help your staff organise, communicate, share, even occasionally grumble. In reality, though, few stray from constructive feedback. Trust in a workforce is rarely misplaced, otherwise there are real problems with the hiring approach. Healthy policies need only encourage the community to tell it like it is, but to keep it constructive. The community will generally remind those who vent or are malicious to stay balanced. Those unconvinced by this new world of openness, were pointed towards the glassdoor website.[1] Here, they saw that staff were already discussing their employers, their salaries and their culture. I suspect that our community of businesses exploring the benefits of social alignment was self-selecting because most were actually encouraged by the experience as they scanned comments like, 'The work is challenging and rewarding,' or 'a diverse culture and good training', or even on one occasion, 'Great management team.' However, there were some winces around the room to comments like 'Quick to pile on the responsibility, slow to recognise' or 'culture of mediocrity', as they realised that staff in any company were rating their employers as candidly as they would review a hotel on TripAdvisor. What was most unexpected was that interviewees were ranking their interviewers with comments like, 'HR ran through the questions quickly without listening,' and 'didn't bother to respond for four weeks'. It would be a mistake to dismiss these reviews as entirely motivated by rejection. We have all come to naturally weigh the motivation of a reviewer in our final analysis and look beyond individual comments for patterns. One interviewee complained that he was 'disappointed

---

1   http://www.glassdoor.com.

with the interviewers', feeling that they 'lacked the capacity to think laterally'. That might be a red flag for other talented engineers thinking about applying to that company. They are unlikely to refuse an interview, but they will arrive ready to check for themselves. In a world where both sides of an interview can share their views with the world, it's not clear who should be working hardest to create the best impression. The illustrations are powerful. Control, no. Listening, yes.

Listening Outside

The predominant use of social listening outside the organisation is to collect and filter 'mentions', instances of an organisation, company, individual, brand, product or marketing campaign being referenced in an item of online content. Mentions, combined with sentiment, help us to understand what customers really think of a brand and what staff really think about the company.

But there are many other uses. Social listening is a key component of *social customer relationship management* (sCRM) or *social selling*. It would more accurately be called 'social buying', because, in truth the shift to selling in this way is as a result of the change in buying behaviours. Customers have access to much more information. They will educate themselves, research, evaluate and poll their own trusted network long before they involve a seller. By the time they reach out to a supplier, they expect it to be as informed about the business they are selling to as they are about the company they are buying from – that is to say, extraordinarily so.

Professor Derek A. Newton of the Darden School at the University of Virginia suggested that professional sellers have evolved through four stages: music man, animated catalogue, magic formula and problem-solver. Before the First World War, the charismatic music man charmed customers into buying. After the First World War, the animated catalogue delivered well-rehearsed presentations covering every feature and function. This approach, well suited to selling vacuum cleaners, was superseded in the 1930s by the magic formula. The magic was a series of predetermined steps that the seller need only walk the customer through to be sure of a sale at the end. Today, sellers are required to be more consultative. Their customers expect them to listen, to understand their problems and to help solve them. Social sellers need to be armed with information from both traditional and social sources. Enlightened sellers will set up listening triggers for the clients they have or are looking to cultivate a relationship with. These alerts represent opportunities to get to know the customer better. They might even be events that indicate that a client or prospective client needs their help immediately – mutual and timely opportunities to both serve and to sell. A customer entering a new territory may need local assistance. A business that has just acquired a new company might need help merging multiple customer databases. A sustainability award might indicate that the winning company would be interested in your own recent innovations in green products or services. Those on a growth curve might be on the hunt for talent, and those in difficult markets might be interested in any solution that will help them do more with less. In all cases, an educated customer expects their suppliers to have taken as much interest in them as they have in their suppliers.

More generally, social listening can be about understanding a market. How successful are competitors, what new consumer behaviours are emerging, what is the status of new legislation, and what will its impact be? A retail banking operation might want to monitor competitor interest rates on savings products, public sentiment on offshore call centres or the changes in senior roles in regulatory bodies. Applications for social listening are as varied as those for human listening, with the exception that a social listening platform can hear millions of conversations.

From Listening to Information

In previous chapters we have discussed the changing nature of data – a shift from transactional behaviours recorded in transactional systems to genuine interactions largely understood through unstructured sources of information, often representing human conversation. Transactional data from a process, say a customer purchase, are recorded in a highly structured form with a customer number, date, product and price. These data are stored in columns that can be analysed later along with all the other customer transactions to spot, for example, trends in customer and product profitability. Similarly, HR transactional systems record when people start and when they leave, and usually categorise their reason for leaving. Detail and completeness is sacrificed in the interest of expedient systems engineering. The employee leaving was avoidable or unavoidable, and the reason will be one of a short list, including things like 'left for better package', 'left for better position', 'performance-related' or 'redundant role'. The transactional recording of this data is only as detailed as the designers of the system felt it needed to be. If there was little perceived value in capturing other reasons, perhaps a long commute, then this isn't recorded. Further, if the reason was only partially about the package but also about the quality of work, then a decision will be made, perhaps arbitrarily, about the primary reason. The process of analysing this type of data, while requiring some restructuring, is relatively straightforward and offers useful, if sometimes broad, insights. We could, for example, determine how many people left for a better package, but we would not know how many times this was variable pay versus basic pay because the system chose not to record this level of details. It fell outside the transaction.

Conversely, human conversations are rich, filled with information, and given time, much more complete. The HR manager will leave an exit interview with a real sense of why the employee left, what it was about the package, their manager, the culture or the company as a whole that failed to retain them. A full-text transcript of the exit interview then would be a complete record of the exit event, but text is not data. Words can be ambiguous. For example, 'design' can be a noun or a verb and 'ladders' and 'ceilings' can apply to both buildings and careers. Sentences can also be ambiguous. The sentence 'I heard my colleague on the phone' doesn't tell us whether the colleagues were both on the phone or whether one overheard the other. Text and conversations are also reliant on context. The sentence 'Sue started walking to work' tells us that Sue once commuted some other way, perhaps using public transport, and that Sue lives within walking distance to the office.

It isn't just words, sentences and grammar that are ambiguous. Rich and intricate human communication is inherently imprecise and open to many interpretations. The couple in Ira Gershwin's song 'Let's Call The Whole Thing Off' are a good example of how language can get in the way of discourse. They lament the way they pronounce the same words differently because it exposes class differences which might eventually result in the end their relationship. Interestingly, if they had met on Facebook today, then regardless of how they pronounced 'neither', 'either' and 'tomato', they would have assumed that they, like the spelling, were a perfect match.

The Trouble with Social Listening

Understanding nuance in human communication is a preoccupation for those innovating in the field of social listening. It is the point at which the vast sea of blog, editorial and social content is collected and prepared for usable analysis as information. Listening platforms not only need to deal with extraordinary volumes, but the human capacity for saying the same thing in many different ways. Fred Astaire and Ginger Rogers were both speaking (American) English, and yet still had problems because language is only one of the many considerations when we try to understand the written word. Slang, regional idioms and differences in style relating to social groupings, profession, generation and gender are just a few others.

Anyone with teenage children can tell you about generational language differences. One obtuse example is the use of the expression 'pwned' as in 'You just got pwned' or 'She pwned me' – usually, but not exclusively, when playing video and computer games. It describes the process of being decisively and unambiguously beaten by a competitor. One headline on the website The Cult of Mac in April 2012 read: 'Why Apple Has Already Pwned the Gaming Market'. 'Pwned' is a corruption of 'owned' attributed to a misspelling by a map designer working on the online role-playing game World of Warcraft map, and for some reason it fell into common usage.

Unlike much of what we deal with in information systems, there is no rule, no derivation, it is simply something which is known. Without this knowledge, what would a social media monitoring platform make of the tweet 'coke pwnd pepsi during Superbowl' (or the other way round, of course)?

There are other equally arbitrary differences between age groups. In a networked world, tribal communication can take hold quickly. A cursory look at the website Urban Dictionary will demonstrate the wealth of phraseology that might be understood by gen-Yers (born 1980–1999), possibly by a gen-Xer (born early 1960s–1980), but less likely by a boomer (born 1946–1964). For example, a 'First World injury' is one that can only occur in a highly developed economy, such as walking into a lamp post while texting on a smartphone. Some phrases apply to very specific circumstances, like 'business casualty' – an instance of someone dressing inappropriately or poorly when the office dress code is 'business casual'. Another, 'powerstreaming', refers to watching an entire season of a television show in a row, usually on a streaming service like Apple TV or Netflix. Others have broader application, like the phrase 'Stupid Tax', which refers to government-supported lotteries. Even emoticon usage differs by age group, apparently. Baby boomers rarely use them, gen-Xers commonly use them, and gen-Yers use them, but differently. A gen-Xer is more likely to use :-) whereas a gen-Yer would use :) – very little difference to the human eye, but in computer-based text, filters they simply don't match.

Many are a little surprised when I point out that the author's gender makes a difference to the language used. Of course, women may be more likely to discuss hormone replacement therapies and men more likely to discuss male-pattern baldness if they are blogging about their mid-life crisis, but given a gender-neutral topic, men and women still use different language. One Web app, BookBlog's Gender Genie,[2] can identify the gender of the author of a piece of text with a surprisingly high degree of accuracy. What does all of this mean? It means that social media analytics platforms have to understand the rich, inconsistent and unfathomable ways in which we all converse. To be more specific and technical, social listening must employ linguistic variant sets to accurately disambiguate language variations. Simply put, the tools must be able to handle a set of alternative ways of saying the same thing. Social listening must be inclusive of all diversity, regardless of age, gender, ethnicity, social status, profession and sexuality before it can capture data suitable for the purpose of analytics.

Natural Language Processing and Entity and Topic Extraction

Social listening platforms like Dachis's Social Business Index and others, including Socialmention, Silobreaker, Radian6, Lexalytics and Artesian Insight are able to extract meaning from human conversations using techniques such as natural language understanding and natural language processing (NLP). NLP (not to be confused with neuro-linguistic programming) is the application of linguistics and statistical techniques to extract concepts and patterns from naturally expressed human dialogue. The result is that unstructured text can be understood and analysed in ways similar to structured data. Relationships can be identified, topics can be understood, opinions can be counted, and conversations can be filtered based on their relevance. What people say can be transformed into information, and therefore knowledge, using social listening.

Natural language processing – the transformation of language into information – is a complex process, and is broken up into many individual tasks that give us an insight into how the process works. The principal NLP task is identifying the target of a conversation – the 'who' or 'what' the conversation is actually about. A place, a person, an organisation, company, brand or product? In business, this is typically focused on identifying a brand or a company. This task, Named Entity Recognition (NER) uses linguistic and grammar based models to identify the object of the conversation but even simple word matching reveals that identification of an object is not always straightforward.

---

2   http://bookblog.net/gender/genie.php.

Toyota, Pfizer, Vodafone, Nike, Lego, Toyota, Walmart, HSBC, Disney and Ikea are all unambiguously global brands recognisable by the simplest processing. However, conversations that contain the words 'Apple', 'Amazon', 'Visa' and 'Subway' could be about fruit, rainforests, travel documentation or public transportation rather than global brands. It would be much easier for social listening platforms if the corporate world was populated with companies called Netflix, SocialText and Facebook rather than those named using real words like Next, Gap, Boss and Yell. Likewise, company acronyms court ambiguity. TFL could refer to Transport for London, the TravelFind software product or a Welsh wireless communications business.

The next task is identifying the theme of the conversation. What exactly is the discussion that calls out the Toyota brand about? What is the topic? Is it about the release of a new model, a price increase or a recall? This is what the NLP Task Topic Extraction task will tell us. There are a number of techniques that social platforms use, but the conceptually simplest uses query-based categorisation. If the text contains 'management buy-out', 'employee buy-out', 'takeover', 'merger' or 'acquisition' in close textual proximity to the Named Entity, we know that it is about merger and acquisition. A query-based categorisation would also have to include many variations, including acronyms, synonyms and hyponyms, words or phrases that are more specific – for example, 'white knight' to mean a company making a more acceptable counter-offer for a firm in the middle of a hostile takeover.

Natural conversations don't limit themselves to one topic and one entity. *Topic and entity segmentation*, rather than extraction, refers to the detection of changes of topic or entity in text. Some entities will be incidental. A news article in March 2012 about the CEO of Bristol-Myers Squibb, Lamberto Andreotti, receiving a pay rise also includes comments from spokeswoman Jennifer Mauer. The article's topic, a CEO's pay rise, means that the reference to Mauer is only incidental.

Data Extraction

Conversations can also contain those things that we naturally regard as data – the temperature in a city on a certain date, the price of a product, the salary level of a job posting. Conversations and other online content can contain email addresses, dates, product names, contributors and authors. A news article will be published on a date, by an author, in a category, with a title, a summary and then the article text itself. To the human reader, these are data points, but to the computer they are all text. You can try this for yourself. On a Web page displaying a news article, select the 'View Source' option available in most Web browsers. You will quickly get a sense that while we think of these as identifiable pieces of data, there is no such indication in the source. The source you are looking at is HTML, the common language of browsers, and illustrates the general limitations of text published on the Web today. It is all just text, not data. It is understandable to a reader, but unintelligible to a computer for any purpose other than display. In fact, the purpose of HTML is to determine how text, pictures and other media are displayed. It communicates no meaning. The HTML surrounding the headline 'Bahrain Protester Found Dead on Eve of Grand Prix' contains information about the font style, colour and size, but nothing to denote that it is the headline of an article. Text analytic products, a superset of social listening products, have to derive the fact that this text is a headline from analysing the text using relative positioning and other textual 'clues'.

From Text to Analytics

In just these few NLP tasks we can determine from a social or other online source the topic of the conversation, who or what the conversation is about, the sentiment and a number of data points. Our human conversation is beginning to exhibit some of the characteristics of data. There are many more NLP tasks, though. These include relationship extraction – for example, that a piece of text refers to Bristol-Myers, its CEO and its spokesperson. The same article also refers to the Securities and Exchange Commission, the regulatory body with which Bristol-Myers is obliged to file its financial statements. These are all relationships which can help to understand the nature of the entities referred to in the text.

These and other NLP tasks, including disambiguation and automatic summarisation, transform unstructured text into information that can be understood by a machine. It can be analysed, it can be the subject of social analysis.

Conclusion

Listening is an essential skill in human communication. Until now, computers, and specifically the Internet, have not been locuses of interaction, let alone listening. Unlike Frasier Crane, computers are not good listeners. Human language is imprecise and ambiguous. It requires context, reasoning and understanding. The field of computer science that is dealing with this, natural language processing, is evolving quickly. Services that can identify which company the conversation is about, the broad topic of the conversation and the overall sentiment exist today. The issue of imprecision is being addressed all the time, but today the sheer volume of conversations being analysed means that the levels of accuracy are surprisingly high. In fact, the approach is already challenging traditional equivalents like opinion polls and consumer surveys.

As we have seen consistently, this technology for listening and understanding has so far been focused on customers of consumer businesses (B2C) The applications for business to business (B2B) and inside the firewall are equally exciting. Organisational conversations can be understood, and questions can be asked and answered in natural language. At last, the organisation can unambiguously make the claim that it is listening.

SENTIMENT EXTRACTION

Sentiment extraction has generated the most interest and investment in the field of NLP. Assuming that the entity is a company or a brand, there is real and obvious value in understanding the sentiment of the conversation. Social listening, though, has to deal with any number of issues before sentiment is understood.

Take, for example, a random set of conversations about the 2012 movie, *The Artist*. In this example, we have extracted sample text from the micro blogging service Twitter in the form of tweets. The sentiments of some tweets are obvious. Take, for example, the following tweet from @Oscar_Ruiz, which is unambiguously positive:

> *Having a Great night of Movies and popcorn watching #TheArtist*
> *Im loving this film :) #SaturdayNight*

A tweet from @MissVeeBW is negative, but a human reader would detect that this is without even seeing the film:

> #TheArtist I think I know what to expect. From experience these movies that r all the rage at #Cannes r usually a snorefest

@arvinmirador is also clearly feeling positive to the film, but the sentiment is directed towards the lead actor, Jean Dujardin, rather than the movie:

> #jeandujardin is to die for in #theartist killer smile. Simply dashing :)

Some tweets express no obvious sentiment, so are clearly neutral, like this one from @luxuryscript which reads simply:

> watching #TheArtist

or this one from The Roxy Theatre, @RoxySaskatoon:

> Opening Friday, April 27th at The Roxy: #BeingFlynn and #TheArtist-- #yxe #yxefilm #sask @alliancefilms

Some tweets express a mix of sentiment. In this one from @destroface, the negative sentiment is not directed towards the film:

> People who love #TheArtist but despise the new #ThreeStooges are hilarious to me

Some tweets express an ironically negative sentiment in a way that is intended to convey a positive sentiment towards the target of the tweet, like this one from @FarahKhairat:

> After watching #theartist I'm starting to believe that talking is overrated!

Sentiment is important. A study of US and UK companies conducted by the Temkin Group quantified something that is obvious to everyone. Customers are more loyal to companies that treat them properly. Putting numbers to it, though, is important. What the Temkin Group's analysis showed was that a $1 billion company can improve revenues by $140 million–380 million over three years if it improves customers' experiences.

10

Engaged Decisions

For, in the end, it is impossible to have a great life unless it is a meaningful life. And it is very difficult to have a meaningful life without meaningful work.

Jim Collins, Good to Great

SIGNPOSTS

- ✓ The economic value of aligning individual decisions to strategic ones
- ✓ How good decisions require engaged employees
- ✓ Why managers and corporate culture can be barriers to engagement
- ✓ How activity streams provide an alternative to endless rules and bureaucracy
- ✓ How the agile social enterprise engages everyone in decision making

Big Decisions Require Aligned Small Ones

Jeff Bezos doesn't want you talking to Amazon. He believes that if you're speaking to his company on a weekend, you're wasting time you could be spending talking to your friends and family. Amazon's customer service strategy is to cater for its customers online, 100 per cent of the time, with no customer service calls. It's a refreshing approach to anyone who has spent 20 minutes holding for their Internet service provider. Bezos expresses his vision vividly. It's implemented, though, through Amazon's website design, through the content in its online help, through the packaging, handling and shipping of each and every customer order. Strategic decisions about the customer experience made by a few are implemented through the willing participation of many. Big decisions are made manifest by hundreds of smaller ones. Great customer service isn't provided by poorly motivated staff, it comes from those who are enthusiastic, diligent, well-trained and properly rewarded. Organisations that will survive and ideally thrive in an era of unprecedented change will not do so because of their procedures or their policy manual. By the time the documents have been approved and circulated, their business will have moved on. More than ever before, companies need their people to feel involved in order to be engaged.

However, it appears that few have achieved this. Two Towers Watson Global Workforce Studies in 2009 and 2012 paint a picture of anything but engagement. Organisations, it seems, are committed to empowerment and engagement as rhetoric, not as a reality. The 2009 survey, the largest of its kind, took responses from almost 90,000 respondents in 18 countries and identified that almost 80 per cent of staff are, at best, only partially engaged. Almost half of this group actually described themselves as 'disengaged'. The 2012 study showed little improvement with almost two thirds describing themselves as disengaged, detached or unsupported. Business activity, the hierarchy, the procedures, the performance appraisals, the management model are failing to connect us to the work we do. And many in the workforce don't even trust their managers. Only a little over a third of workers believed that managers were genuinely interested in their wellbeing, and a similar minority believed that managers communicated openly and honestly.

Engagement Cannot be Bought

Our employers pay our mortgages, feed our families and may pay health insurance premiums, but money cannot buy everything, it seems. Workers are disaffected. They are not committed to the very companies that are the basis of their livelihoods. They are uninterested in an institution which has had profound positive sociological and economic consequences for all of us. In the developed world, our supermarket shelves are piled high with produce from around the globe. Our vacations are spent in corners of the planet accessible only because of commercial airlines. This book was written on a device which required research and development far in excess of any individual pocket, and distributed both physically and digitally on a foundation laid down as a result of major capital investments. The corporation has made the impossible possible. At its worst, though, it keeps us hanging on the phone, waiting at home for an unkept appointment, and leaves us stranded in departure lounges. Much worse, an unchecked profit motive can destroy livelihoods, neighbourhoods, environments and lives. Examples are, sadly, all too easy to find: Philip Morris releasing research from a study outlining the positive financial implications of smokers' deaths for the Czech government; the chronic erosion of ethics at News Corp. that resulted in police and government investigations into phone hacking, bribery and corruption. As this book is being written, the global economy is enduring a slow and uncertain recovery after the financial services sector gorged itself on trillions of dollars' worth of toxic credit default swaps that brought about the worst financial crisis since the 1930s. At their worst, corporations – entities treated legally as if they were people – can be tough to love. Joel Bakan, author of *The Corporation*, might argue that if a company were a person, it would be suffering from memory loss. Its original intent, to serve people, has been long forgotten. In fact, Bakan argues, its single-minded pursuit of shareholder profit means it has a deeply unpleasant, even psychopathic, personality. If we asked it to take its place on the psychiatrist's couch, the analyst would diagnose childhood psychosis – from 1916, to be precise. A landmark courtroom battle took place in that year between Henry Ford and John Dodge. Dodge, a shareholder in Ford, wanted to finance his own company with his brother from his Ford dividends. Ford felt that the profit levels were steep, even obscene, and wanted to divert dividends back to his customers in the form of a cheaper Model T. Ford argued that business was a 'service not a bonanza', but the Dodge brothers won their case. The judges' ruling in *Dodge* v. *Ford* has become known as the 'best interest of the corporation' principle. Managers and directors have a legal duty to put the shareholders' interest above all others. It's this predisposition to a single purpose – to have no legal obligation to serve any other interest than that of the shareholders – that troubles Bakan. Of course, in a networked world where social mishaps and environmental misdemeanours are covered on 24-hour news, picked over by bloggers, amplified by activists and spread through the Twittersphere in moments, the corporation has become a lot more self-aware. Arguably, though, the reason is still rooted in protecting the share price rather than a regard for people or planet: a slave to the transaction, rather than an active and well-rounded participant in economies, societies, communities and lives.

Purpose: The Price of Better Decisions

It's difficult to make an emotional investment in a corporation if the relationship is going to be so one-sided. Yet we want to. It's a natural human desire to want to be 'part of something', to 'make a difference'. In fact, making a difference, it turns out, is more important than money. Daniel H. Pink, in his book *Drive: The Surprising Truth about What Motivates Us*, draws on decades of scientific research into human motivation and identifies that high performance is not correlated to large amounts of money. One study conducted at MIT involved a large number of students performing a variety of tasks in return for rewards. One group was awarded small, one medium and one large cash incentives. For completely mechanical tasks there was a strong correlation between reward and performance. This was no surprise. However, tasks that involved even the most rudimentary cognitive skill did not follow the same pattern at all – in fact, the larger the reward, the poorer the performance. Top-tier economists from MIT, Carnegie Mellon and the University of Chicago reached a conclusion that flies in the face of the way most companies build their reward and performance management systems. Higher rewards did not lead to better performance. What's more, they repeated the tests in rural India, where the monetary rewards were as high as two months' salary for the participants, with exactly the same results. The group offered the top rewards performed the worst of all. It would appear that the efficacy of carrots and sticks on human motivation is highly questionable. Money is, of course, an important motivation, but only in so far as it needs to be 'enough'. Our engagement, it seems, can't be bought, though. This, according to Pink, stems from three things: purpose, mastery and autonomy. We need to make a difference, we need to get better at doing it, and we want to do it our own way. A business must make profit. But profit is not purpose. The purpose of Apple is to make beautiful products, to delight customers first. Shareholder and other stakeholder benefits follow. The number one focus at Google is the user, and 'all else will follow'. Purpose isn't limited to the desirable, the glamorous and the innovators. Hallmark's business is not built around products; instead, it is built around customer moments. Hallmark wants to enrich lives by helping customers to communicate, connect and celebrate. When I met a group of managers from Tetra Pak, the multinational packaging firm, they mildly rebuked my description of their business. Their company didn't make boxes. Their company made food and drink safe and available everywhere. We can even find meaning in a cup of coffee. Howard Schultz, CEO of Starbucks, wanted to build a company with 'soul'. All employees in the USA who work 20 hours a week receive health cover for themselves and their partners, including unmarried partners. Schultz's father struggled and worked hard all his life, but in poorly paid industries. He never enjoyed health insurance, and didn't even receive compensation when he was hurt at work. Schultz wanted to build a company that respected people, that would have respected his father. Our humanity is not nourished by profit, but by purpose. There is no transaction that concludes in an exchange of human engagement.

Bureaucracy Versus Ambient Awareness and Activity Streams

Bureaucracy is a rational system characterised by clear rules and the systematic allocation of accountability. Its origins are in the work of German sociologist and economist Max Weber, who suggested that the characteristics of an ideal bureaucracy were:

- a hierarchy of authority

- impersonality

- written rules of conduct

- promotion based on achievement

- specialised division of labour

- efficiency.

The bureaucratic co-ordination of the activities of large numbers of people still pervades both public and private organisations. Companies use hierarchy, rules and the division of responsibility to scale while maintaining control; the larger the organisation, the more pervasive the rules and processes. In IBM, the procedures to support a company of some 400,000 staff are affectionately referred to as 'blue-reaucracy'. Weber studied rather than invented bureaucracy. He recognised it as technically efficient, but was also wary of its inadequacies. Rather selectively, Weber wanted to keep a 'portion of mankind' free from this 'parcelling out of the soul'. It lacks humanity, its purpose is to make people as predictable as machines. It flies in the face of a human social group, which is a network of people, not hardware. It is authoritarian, arguably undemocratic and controlling. Few warm to the stewards of bureaucracy either. In extremis, bureaucrats don't see people, they see status. The term 'jobsworth' has fallen into common usage to describe someone who does not see unique circumstances and situations, only rules and process.

To some extent, though, bureaucracy has become accepted as the necessary cost of producing predictable organisational outcomes in the administration of governments and global corporations: the method by which activity conducted by any individual aligns with activity being conducted by the rest of the organisation. It is, to a greater or lesser extent, the default setting for organisational growth. However, there is an alternative to bureaucratic systems of control: an inclusive system of awareness. Trust everyone to do the right thing, guided by core principles, while making everyone aware of what everyone else is doing. If this sounds anarchic, it is, at least partially, because we have never before had an opportunity to keep everyone up to date with the activities of everyone else. This has only been made possible by the rapid growth of the organisational *activity stream*. The activity stream in lifestyle social platforms is the flow of Facebook and LinkedIn status updates. It is the collection of listens, reads, runs, hikes and likes in your group of friends. In an organisation, which is after all a group of people with a common purpose, it has greater significance. It replaces control with awareness. Activity from business systems, customer feedback and personal status are all captured and shared. Updates flow from individual streams to corporate activity streams. Executives openly share their thoughts and latest information, Sales shares the customers it intends to meet, Finance shares which expenses have been approved, engineers share their latest ideas, production planners share their latest finished activity. Sharing is easy, extremely easy. Much of it is frictionless, generated from smart socially integrated systems. Activity streams are not rigid like formal systems, they don't pour like water and set like concrete. Instead, they work how people work. They allow people to express detail about their work or their life as ambient data so that others can listen or so that listening platforms can spot patterns, alert others or identify exceptions.

Activity streams are an open standard, an evolution of Atom and Really Simple Syndication (RSS) feeds which allow us to receive website updates without having to check them manually today. The open standard means that they can be extracted from one system and displayed in another. The standard has been limited, though. They can describe updates from blogs, wikis and websites, but they cannot describe the rich set of activities now possible on social platforms. They don't provide the metadata to describe activities resulting from Flickr, Pandora, Furl, Tumblr, Skyrock, Reddit or YouTube. Activity streams are a description of an action that was taken (the verb) at a point in time by someone or something (the actor) towards another person or thing (the object), sometimes involving digital objects like a wishlist or photo album (the target)

illustration of activity stream model

actor verb object target

This format allows us to describe someone sharing a link, someone following someone else. In fact, there is a standard set of verbs that include 'add friend', 'check in', 'follow', 'like', 'join', 'play', 'post', 'save', 'share', 'tag' and 'update'. Objects include article, audio, bookmark, comment, file, folder, group, list, note, person, photo, place, playlist, product, review, status and video.

Activity streams ensure that there are no islands, no isolated or hidden actions. Everything is open and connected. There are no staccato sign-offs, disconnected approvals and stilted workflows, and no dependency on any individual or single task. Instead, there is a rapid and continuous flow of activity, rather like an ever-functioning corporate nervous system. Activity streams are open to everyone all the time.

Activity Shock and Facilitated Serendipity

Understandably, some are concerned by all this extra content. They fear information overload. The future looks like it will feature yet another inbox, and the current ones are already barely manageable. It is a common complaint, and it is not going to go away. The cost of producing information inside and outside the organisation is so low that it is no longer naturally filtered by the relative cost of producing it. However, according to Clay Shirky, author of *Here Comes Everybody* and *Cognitive Surplus*, the problem is not information overload, it is filter failure. The challenge is not the growing amount of information, it is the primitive way in which we separate out what we need from what we don't. The social tools that plug us into the corporate consciousness are smart, and are getting smarter at this. They help filter out the noise and strengthen the signal. Not everyone need 'follow' everyone else. Everyone might follow the CEO because her status updates provide insight into strategic direction. She might not follow everyone else, but may take time out to listen to an open activity stream to understand the mood of the business. The activity stream can be routinely filtered but perpetually open as a persistent record of corporate actions.

We shouldn't get hung up on activity streams being just another inbox. They are very different. Email carries an unspoken social contract that responsibility for the next action is completed when it leaves an outbox and is passed on, like the baton in a relay race, to someone else's inbox. This is not the case with activity streams. They are ever-present, but like a Twitter stream, there is no social obligation to read and respond to every post. Instead, they are a searchable social layer that glues the whole organisation together. Adaptable and flexible, they cut down the need for meetings, reduce email and eliminate duplicated effort.

Finally, in a world of telepresence, videoconferences, global peer groups and home working, the activity stream is a place where happy accidents can happen. It can facilitate (if we tolerate the oxymoron briefly) serendipity – coffee machine moments, kitchen catch-ups and water cooler connections that can result in coincidental connections that extend the network, solve problems in unexpected ways or generate completely new ideas. In their book *Get Lucky*, Thor Muller and Lane Becker describe how chance encounters that happen outside our usual team structures can result in something new and valuable to the organisation. They describe how when Sergey Brin was asked at the Web 2.0 Summit in San Francisco what he attributed Google's incredible success to, the audience were silenced by his response. Brin responded confidently that 'The number one factor that contributed to our success was luck.' Brin was not being glib or modest. He was acknowledging that for any endeavour to succeed with the speed and scale that Google did required more than any one person or single team can ever take responsibility for. It required creative input, diverse opinions and wild ideas that took the organisation in unplanned but ultimately successful directions. Again, this feels counter-intuitive because alignment starts with clear direction. However, there is a certain degree of serendipity in even the clearest visions. Nokia began as a paper mill, PayPal was originally intended to beam electronic IOUs from PalmPilot to PalmPilot, Flickr emerged out of a massively multiplayer online game, and Twitter was going to be a podcasting business. This happens so frequently that there is a name for it. Eric Ries, author of *The Lean Startup*, called the phenomenon 'pivoting'.

Facilitated serendipity is not even limited to being at the same water cooler at the same time. Like conversations on Twitter, individuals don't need to be in the same place at the same time to talk about the same thing. Take a look at the hashtags #Howtomakepeoplemad or #somethingIgetalot on Twitter, and the conversations span days and time zones. What's more, they are inclusive. All are welcome. You will only be valued on your contribution, not your status. Activity streams can enable good ideas to be heard, but more importantly, unconstrained by time and space, they can grow.

Alignment: A Source of Economic Value

Organisational alignment is critically important, but hard to carry off. When strategic decisions are made, a team of 50, 500 or 50,000 need to pull in the same direction. In their book *Alignment*, Robert S. Kaplan and David P. Norton liken alignment to the eight-person shells that they regularly see racing up the Charles River separating Boston and Cambridge, Massachusetts. If the eight athletes each did their own thing, their shell could slow to a halt, circle or capsize. The winning crew, they observe, 'invariably row in beautiful synchronism'. Corporate alignment creates the same outcome: many individuals getting behind each decision with the commitment and energy to move at speed. The analogy can be stretched too far, though. The objectives of a company are many, the path winding and the decisions complex, often requiring trade-offs. In an ever-changing market that requires continuous innovation, alignment requires that the 'crew' be consulted often to get its input to ensure the best possible decisions. Once the decision is made, then the team has to be committed to acting upon it. Even those who held alternative views need to feel sufficiently bought-in to give the decision the best possible chance of success. Alignment when decisions are passed down through the hierarchy is at a distinct disadvantage. These are edicts; formal proclamations that, at their worst, can be poorly communicated, even inexplicable. They can be the equivalent of a tense parent tersely commanding, 'Because I told you so.'

Control Versus Participation

Sergey Brin and Larry Page were both born in 1972. Google was started when they met at Stanford University, and was incorporated in 1998. Both attended Montessori schools, which encourage children to discover rather than be instructed, and to make their own choices. The teachers don't make decisions about the morning or afternoon activities, the children do. My own son attended a Montessori school, to which I partly credit the smooth ride we had through his teenage years, because self-discipline and independence are at Montessori's core. This must have all been radical when Maria Montessori opened her first classroom in 1907 in a tenement building in Rome. Family decisions were probably made by one person, and while it might have been a matriarchy or a patriarchy in Italy, it certainly did not involve the children. Today, Montessori principles do not seem too far off centre. The generation entering the workplace today have been consulted and involved in family decisions. They had a say in the type of birthday party they wanted, what cut of jeans they wore and which destination they preferred for a day out. Family decisions have been made as a team, not at the centre. It has not, in my experience, been easy. In fact, it has been harder, but the results immeasurably better. Workplaces have also evolved. When I entered the workplace, decisions were centralised, and management styles authoritarian. Today, important decisions are increasingly made by teams, peer groups, special interest groups, councils and the staff that are impacted.

The evolving family dynamic has entered the workplace. Many of the characteristics of Brin and Page's Montessori education are in evidence in the Google corporate culture. Google encourages everyone to share ideas and opinions, and at their weekly all-hands meetings, anyone can question the decisions the organisation has made. The founding ten 'truths' of Google include 'You can make money without doing evil' and 'You can be serious without a suit.' It represents a growing shift away from decisions through hierarchy, authority and bureaucracy.

Inclusive Decision Making is No Longer Exclusive

Google isn't even at the most progressive end of corporate culture. Brighton-based social business pioneer NixonMcInnes is recognised as one of the most democratic workplaces in the world. The bank balance and financial accounts are open to everyone in the company, and that includes payroll. Discussing each others' salaries at software giant EDS was a dismissible offence when I consulted for it in the 1980s; at NixonMcInnes they are common knowledge. Pay and rations are not decided by the hierarchy either. A decentralised Rewards Team decides, based on principles of fairness, equity and affordability. All pay is reviewed by this function, even that of the founders.

Such thinking is not limited to avant-garde consultancies in creative cloisters of the United Kingdom. HCL technologies is an IT solutions provider to the manufacturing sector with 90,000 employees and revenues of $3 billion, operating in more than 25 countries. Its CEO, Vineet Nayar, has turned the hierarchy upside down. Management and managers are accountable to those who create the value: staff hire the boss. The result, according to Nayar in an *IndustryWeek* article, *Employees First, Customers Second* published in February 2012, is that 'it unleashes the power of the many and loosens the stranglehold of the few. It increases the speed and quality of innovation and decision-making where it matters most'.

Gary Hamel is acknowledged by *Fortune* magazine as the world's leading expert on business strategy. In his book *What Matters Now*, Hamel seems genuinely disappointed that most large companies operate the same ritual of goal-setting, planning, budgeting and performance appraisals. Businesses seem to compete largely by aping each others' processes. There is even less variety, Hamel observes, in the architecture of power. It is only the fringe, the market challengers and the avant-garde, that shun the status quo. However, when Hamel visited Gore, he discovered that the radical can be found in the most ordinary of companies. The company is best known for its Gore-Tex range of products. Its high-performance products have probably kept you comfortable and dry on at least one trek, bike ride or climb at some point in your life. As innovative as Gore-Tex products are, they couldn't, in a sense, be more ordinary – boots and coats.

There is no hierarchy at Gore, its CEO Terri Kelly explained in an interview with Hamel. Decisions don't have to make their way up to the top and back down again. Instead, Kelly went on: 'we're a lattice or a network, not a hierarchy, and associates can go directly to anyone in the organisation to get what they need to be successful'. An organisation which resists job titles, where everyone is an owner and leadership is determined based on the willingness of others to follow, sounds like a haven for the work-shy. Democratic principles are all very worthy, but surely the more people that are involved in a decision, the longer it takes to make? Hamel focused on this very question with Kelly, asking: 'I can understand how this painstaking consultation produces buy-in, but doesn't it slow things down?' Kelly was frank and candid in his reply. The decision making process can be frustrating. However, Kelly explained, the payback is great: 'If you spend more time up front, you'll have associates who are not only fully bought in but committed to achieving the outcome.' Kelly continued: 'Along the way, they'll also help to refine the idea and make the decision even better.' Hamel was quick to highlight the time invested in traditional top-down decision making after the decision is made. Senior managers spend time selling a decision once it has been made in an attempt to achieve alignment. Traditional companies achieve alignment through positioning the decision and creating financial incentives through a shared scorecard. Gore arrives at its decisions with alignment baked in. If further validation is needed, then look to their commercial success. Founded in 1958, the business has never made a loss.

Cultural implications aside, inclusive decision making has been limited by practicalities. W.L. Gore, for example, never lets its plants grow beyond 150–200 people before creating a new one. Functionally, it is difficult to poll groups, obtain their input, collate their views, share opinions and establish a consensus without committees, sub-committees and employee councils. It has been a challenge to distribute information. It has been difficult to collaborate around the hard numbers needed to make a decision. It has been impractical to organise and align the needs of the business, its stakeholders and those who participate in the business as employees and partners. Social platforms have changed all of this. They have removed the barriers. Concerned constituents can be reached regardless of their department, function, office or geography. They don't need to be in the same building, company or country. Once involved, social platforms make collaboration easy. As Shirky puts it in his book *Here Comes Everybody*: 'Whenever you improve a group's ability to communicate internally, you change the things it is capable of.'

Inclusive decision making in the family is creating a generation of independent thinkers. They enter the workforce expecting to be consulted, and are predisposed to share responsibility for the outcomes of those decisions, good or bad. This means a growth in engagement in successful outcomes within organisations from a much broader group than ever before.

The Sharing Motivation

If an organisation has everything to gain from the highest levels of participation in decision making, so do the people that make up the organisation. We want to create, to participate, to be involved and share our ideas. There is a fundamental human need to connect and to share. Even in an environment where ideas are 'currency', the default is better open than closed. Take for example, television programme ideas that can launch careers. In Euan Semple's book *Organisations Don't Tweet, People Do*, Semple describes them as 'gold dust'. When someone posted a programme idea on an open forum, Semple, then BBC Director of Knowledge Management, recalled: 'You could almost hear the collective intake of breath at such a rash act'. Eventually, someone commented on the post and asked whether the poster wasn't concerned that someone else could claim the idea as their own. According to Semple, it didn't take long for someone to post that there could be very little doubt over the provenance of an idea posted, date-stamped and shared with 25,000 witnesses.

One organisation, a large restaurant chain in the UK that participated in our regular Social Business Briefings, places a similar premium on ideas. It operates in a highly competitive market, its appeal is broad, and its typical spend per head is low, leaving little room for error. To be able to deliver consistent quality and maintain brand value demands equally consistent operational performance. Ultimately, its success is determined by the hundreds of decisions each of its restaurant managers make on a daily basis. Do they have enough staff each night to ensure that service is attentive? Is the shift overstaffed to a point where is will hurt profitability? Are they promoting the right offers? Are they maintaining levels of quality that are consistent with the brand? Successful managers are ones who make the most of the brand and adapt to the specifics of their location. Perhaps, if the location is next to a cinema, staff may be trained to advise customers what items on the menu are quickest to prepare and to keep a constant eye on the clock, ensuring that diners have just enough time for a relaxed three courses and coffee. Location dynamics are not necessarily static, either. If road or building work means that traffic does not flow by the front door, then the best managers will invest in temporary signage to make sure they don't miss their passing customers. Each subtle way in which a manager influences how the restaurant is run – a serial stream of ideas – can make the difference between moderate and high performance. Over time, a manager who makes all the right decisions, implements all the right ideas, sees them turn into profit, and it's the profit that gets noticed. Over a period of months and quarters, even a small number of years, those increased profits start to look like success. Successful managers gain recognition and rewards, and eventually promotion, perhaps to regional management, taking on responsibility for a group of restaurants.

Keen to continue their success, newly promoted regional managers will look to scale their success by replicating the practices behind it with managers in their region. At this point, the patterns of successful decisions and ideas are unlocked for the first time. As a restaurant manager, not only were the opportunities to share limited, but there was no motivation. Indeed, if the manager continued to operate the set of practices without sharing, then the likelihood that the resulting performance would make them stand out from the crowd might be a motivation not to share. The practices that result in good decision making are shared much later than the point at which it is becoming evident that they are successful. Instead, they are typically shared at the point where they deliver value to the sharer. This can translate into months of lost value for organisations. Social platforms capture the ideas much sooner. Their financial outcomes can be tested, but the originating decision is time-stamped and the author credited automatically. The impetus for sharing good working practices and ideas has shifted. The earlier the idea is shared, the more likely it is that the author will be credited. The earlier the idea is exposed, the sooner it can be implemented by the organisation, increasing the maximum possible value.

Conclusion

Management pioneers Robert Kaplan and David Norton describe alignment as a source of economic value. Alignment needs our engagement. It requires that the hundreds of decisions made by thousands of workers each day are true to the strategic direction of the business. A corporation needs capital to operate, and people need money to live. These facts are inescapable. The paradox, though, is that we are motivated by purpose, not profit. Decades of research support this. Human engagement does not have a price, it is a consequence of opportunity for growth, autonomy and the knowledge that we are making a difference.

Traditional companies attempt to manufacture alignment through top-down controls, measurement and reward systems. They are still trying to solve outdated problems of scaling large volumes of workers to perform manual tasks predictably and efficiently. They employ bureaucratic systems of rules, controls and approvals to make a large group of individuals behave like a machine; the larger the company, the more bureaucratic it is, and the more complex the measurement systems. There are new challenges, though. Jack Welch once said that if the rate of change outside a company exceeds the rate of change on the inside, the end is near. Well, the rate of change has never been greater. We need only look at the music industry. That noise in the news is not the death throes of a market, it is the reluctant straining of industry behemoths adapting too slowly. The music business is actually growing. More people are spending more money on more music. While the large record labels perpetuated the myth that their industry was in a downward, piracy-driven, spiral, the global music market grew from $132 billion in 2005 to $168 billion in 2010. However, this growth is being driven by innovators, by independent labels, by digital music pioneers – by those adapting to change, not lobbying against it.

Socially aligned businesses are resilient. They can adapt because they see profits as a consequence of meeting the ever-changing needs of customers, rather than as their purpose. They implement information systems to allow everyone to make the right decision, not out of a desire to control. They adopt social platforms to make everyone aware of activity being conducted by everyone else. Socially aligned companies eschew control and cascading carrots, and replace them with information, interaction and purpose. As a consequence, their decisions are inclusive. Alignment is baked in from the beginning, not sold at the end. Their workforces are motivated, creative and adaptable. And they absolutely need to be, because customers need great service, innovative solutions, and it's all going to change tomorrow. So keep up!

11

Decision Sourced

*One of the great mysteries of large distributed systems, from communities
and organizations to brains and ecosystems, is how globally coherent
activity can emerge in the absence of centralized authority or control.*

Paul Hartzog

SIGNPOSTS

- ✓ How successful businesses engender a 'hero' culture
- ✓ Why inclusive decisions are better-informed and more creative
- ✓ Clearing up the confusion between consensus and collaboration
- ✓ How broad-participation decision making is made possible by social

---

The Heroic Decision Maker

Rudolph (Rudy) Giuliani was mayor of New York from 1994 to 2001. At the
time he was inaugurated, according to Giuliani's own blog, New York City was
averaging five murders and over a thousand serious crimes each and every
day. In 1993 there were 35 murders in a single neighbourhood, Harlem, and
93 in nearby Crown Heights, the scene of rioting two years earlier. By the new
millennium, there were five and 35 respectively, and overall crime fell by over
50 per cent. I have visited New York many times over the last twenty years,
and there is no doubt that the city is a different, safer and more pleasurable
place to visit. Giuliani largely attributes the dramatic decline in crime to his
zero-tolerance, 'broken windows' approach to policing. 'Broken windows'
policing is an aggressive focus on relatively minor offences like vandalism,
metro fare dodging and possession of cannabis. It also doesn't tolerate the
type of begging that involves dragging a filthy sponge over a car windscreen
and then demanding payment before the traffic lights turn green again. I have

seen Giuliani speak about his time as New York's 107th mayor twice, once in the USA and once at a conference in London In 2004. It's a fascinating and compelling story of one man's leadership changing the character of an entire city.

Terry Leahy became CEO of Tesco in 1997. During the year when a hair care product first told us that 'We're worth it,' Tesco had 568 stores and generated £650 million in profits. By 2011, Tesco had almost five times more stores selling the UK its groceries, electronics and homeware, to the tune of £3.1 billion profit. It's a story of one man leading a company to become the UK's number one retailer. During this period, Leahy has been recognised as Business Leader of the Year (2003), European Businessman of the Year (2004) and most influential non-elected person in Britain (2007). He was, most significantly, knighted in 2002, and throughout his tenure the UK press applauded Leahy with headlines including 'Tesco Triumphs Under Sir Terry' and 'How Tesco Chief Changed the Way Britain shops'.

Stories like these grab our attention. Intricate accounts of how public institutions or businesses are transformed into market-beating, even world-beating, organisations are somehow more understandable when we bring them down to the human size of individual achievement. Jack Welch transformed GE, Steve Jobs made Apple the most valuable company in the world, and Jeff Bezos reinvented reading. They make compelling stories. Leaders are revered, frequently quoted, and their decisions endowed with what is often retrospectively ascribed wisdom. Their stories make equally compelling movies. Aaron Sorkin's screenplay for *The Social Network* was so rich, the dialogue so well-crafted in its depiction of Mark Zuckerberg and the rise of Facebook, that when he and director David Fincher realised they couldn't fit it all into the running time of the movie, they asked Jesse Eisenberg, playing Zuckerberg, to just talk faster. We love heroes.

But transformational turnaround in a city where there are almost nine million people, 800 languages and half a million businesses is unlikely to be as simple as a three-act screenplay with a single protagonist calling all the shots. Cities and organisations are complex systems involving groups, crowds, populations and millions of interactions. The actors are all influenced by each other and the environment around them. For example, it may have been demographics rather than policy that made New York safer. Steven Levitt and Stephen Dubner, in their book *Freakonomics*, attribute the free fall in New York's crime rates to social change. Most significant, in their thinking, was the legalisation of abortion in the 1970s. Safe abortions for socially disadvantaged women in the city's poorest districts in the 1970s meant far fewer disenfranchised 18–24-year-old men – the group most likely to commit crime – in the 1990s. Or so the theory goes. It is controversial and not without its detractors, but it doesn't seem any less a credible hypothesis than the sweat, inspiration and perfect decision making prowess of one man. From mayors to CEOs. Jim Collins, author of *Good to Great*, sees leadership as a modern construct that has yet to go through its age of enlightenment. In the sixteenth century, when we didn't understand something like a crop failure we ascribed it to God. Collins argues that: 'in the 20th and 21st Century, when we are looking at the social world, the man-made world, we are still in the dark ages. This is shown by our predilection for looking for leadership answers.'

Vineet Nayar, CEO of HCL, an Indian company referred to as having the world's most modern management model by David Kirkpatrick in *Fortune* magazine, believes that 'the concept of the CEO, the notion of the visionary, the captain of the ship is bankrupt'. Terry Leahy clearly has what Collins believes is a key ingredient in leadership: humility. Leahy himself attributes much of his success to one decision – the introduction of the Tesco Clubcard. In an interview for *Director* magazine, Leahy describes it as 'pivotal', helping Tesco by 'knowing more about what the market was thinking than anyone'. Leahy ranks customer insight through analytics ahead of his own personal decisions. The Tesco Clubcard programme is actually a partnership between Tesco and dunnhumby, an innovator in 'relevance marketing' founded in 1989 which launched the Clubcard scheme with Tesco in 1995. Today, there are hundreds of people within Tesco running the Clubcard in addition to the team at dunnhumby, all of whom have influenced, even made, decisions that led to those additional 2,000 stores.

This isn't to diminish Giuliani or Leahy in any way. Leahy devoted almost two decades of his career to the Tesco business. The journey from his first role in 1979 to CEO in 1997 was no doubt a tough one. Giuliani received an honorary knighthood for his leadership during and after the attacks on the World Trade Center. Their personal achievements and contributions are undeniable. Nor should anyone take lightly the impact of William McKnight on 3M, Yun Jong-Yong on Samsung, Bart Becht on Reckitt Benckiser or George Merck on Merck. It might be argued that the decisions of the average CEO, the wisdom and experience they apply, is 40 times more impactful than that of the average worker – about the same as the pay differential in 1980. It seems unlikely, though, that it is more than 300 times more impactful – the pay differential in 2010.

To attribute organisational success (or failure) to a single leader in this way is simplistic in the extreme. There are so many other corporate factors, market influences and other variables. There are too many other carefully weighed decisions, too much effort, knowledge and experience outside the boardroom; too many other staff, partners, contributors – too many other people.

Decisions Favour the Few

Regardless of the mythology, Leahy and Giuliani did not make decisions alone. We can see that in our own companies. Decisions are made by groups – small ones. They are made by those who are accountable for the outcome, those with key positions of responsibility in the hierarchy, and these are naturally smaller in number. They follow the law of the pyramid: the more important the decision, the higher up the pyramid, the fewer people involved. The degree to which decisions need to be kept confidential rather than public may also constrain participation. However, the pressure being exerted through the increasing adoption of social tools means that privacy and confidentiality are making way for transparency and openness in all cases except where privacy is unequivocally required.

Organisational decisions are not routinely opened out to broad participation through group and crowd decision making. Accountability drives participation. Participation beyond those who are responsible is sparse at best – perhaps domain expertise where it is required, or trusted peers for counsel, and more senior managers for approval. Only decision makers can make decisions. This last sentence is not, as it might first appear, a tautology. When we talk of 'making a decision', it could mean the 'final' decision, or it could refer to the entire process – the 'judgement call', the single step near the end of a decision making process, or the whole process. Making the decision or decision making – it's almost as if because the language doesn't separate these two things, we don't either. We figure that if only a small number of people can make a decision, then only a small number should be involved. Without a clear distinction between decision making and making the decision, we throttle input into the former based on the latter. We don't entertain the notion that many can have input to the decision but only a few – even one – can make the call. We confuse consensus with collaboration. Consensus assumes shared authority to make the call, collaboration does not. Collaborative decisions can accept input regardless of hierarchical position. They can be informed by those who have the knowledge, by opinion from those most affected, by ideas from those closest to the problem.

In fact, in a hyper-connected business, decision makers could harness the power of those connections within the organisation. The command and control characterised by small group decision making could be replaced by collaborative decisions at the opposite end of the spectrum to heroic decision making. The world of collaborative crowdsourcing presents an opportunity to endow the decision with a diverse set of decision alternatives, rigorous analysis and vigorous debate, to improve decisions through a collaboration that sees them enriched with opinion, innovation and knowledge, but not mired in endless meetings or unresolved in an attempt to reach an unattainable consensus.

The Opinionated Crowd

Alfred Sloan Jr became President of General Motors in 1923, and reorganised the company in a way that became the template for modern corporations. He divided the company into autonomous divisions that were lightly managed through financial and policy controls from a small central group. Sloan literally wrote the book on decentralisation, systematic organisation, planning and strategy in one of the first and most influential management publications, *My Years with General Motors*. Things have been more turbulent for GM more recently. In a downward spiral, just prior to its bankruptcy in 2009 and re-listing in 2010, GM was the target of much criticism. David Garvin, a professor at Harvard Business School and author of *Executive Decision Making at General Motors,* a 2004 case study on GM's process for determining policy, suggested that one of the fundamental problems was an inability to make the right strategic call, at least in part because the company had all but eradicated open debate. 'All too many meetings were pre-cooked,' according to Garvin. Executives would line up consensus in pre-meetings to eliminate surprises during regular sessions. This would have dismayed Sloan. He famously postponed a senior executive meeting at GM when his management team nodded their heads when he asked whether they were all in agreement on the decision under consideration. 'Then', he concluded, 'I propose we postpone further discussion until the next meeting to give us time to develop disagreement and perhaps gain some understanding of what the decision is all about.' Surrounded by conviviality and consensus, he instinctively knew that the decision was untested by debate, unchecked by challenge, or perhaps that a better decision had been missed in the absence of alternative viewpoints. While Sloan would not have called it such, the decision was flawed because it had not been subject to a critical social safeguard – *opinion*.

In his book *Management: Tasks, Responsibilities, Practices*, Peter F. Drucker asserts that effective decision makers start with opinions, not with facts. He argues that without opinions one simply finds confirmatory data, and suggests that 'No one has ever failed to find the facts they are looking for.' At first glance, this is counter-intuitive. Drucker, one of the greatest management thinkers of our generation, is suggesting that we do not start with the facts when it comes to decision making. However, Drucker isn't suggesting that decisions be made without data, just that the process should not start with data. Starting with the facts reinforces one-at-a-time decision making and increases the risk of bias, because the information-gathering process will be entirely focused on supporting pre-judgements.

In contrast, leading with opinions opens up possibilities, because opinions are hypotheses, a source of decision alternatives that are, as yet, unclear and untested. By focusing the decision making process on opinions first, a fuller set of decision alternatives is gathered in the form of clarified and tested hypotheses. Safeguarding against confirmation bias only requires inviting the opinions of others; it is a purely social safeguard. According to Clint Eastwood, everyone has opinions, so it follows that every opinion has an owner. Opinion owners are responsible for rounding out their opinions into clear and tested hypotheses.

Drucker signposted additional advantages to opinion-led decision making. Strategic decisions may need new criteria. Traditional criteria and measurement may be the source of the problem or unexploited opportunity, and may only truly be resolved by introducing a fresh perspective in the form of a new opinion. Opinions are often unconstrained and free of organisational pre-conceptions, and can help decision makers be more imaginative in identifying decision alternatives, so they can lead to more creative solutions. Finally decisions are judgements. A balanced decision might entail the selection of a decision alternative that is no more right or wrong than others, therefore the alternatives should be fully understood so that the decision can be both justified and supported.

The Innovative Crowd

Few business leaders would question that the crowd is capable of great ideas. It is a notion as old as the suggestion box. In this regard, we can easily imagine Tesco's staff or their extended community coming up with the idea of a loyalty card to better understand their customers.

We do, however, have a tendency to place too much value on ideas. In his book *ReWork*, Jason Fried has some advice for those with great ideas: start making something. Fried argues that ideas are plentiful, cheap even. If you don't agree, Fried advises, then you should try to sell it and see what you get for it. His point is well made: until a business builds a product or service and convinces others to pay for it, an idea is just that. To quote Mark Zuckerberg spelling it out to the Winklevosses, or more accurately, to quote Aaron Sorkin's screenplay: 'You know, you really don't need a forensics team to get to the bottom of this. If you guys were the inventors of Facebook, you would have invented Facebook.'

Nevertheless, businesses have become disconnected from their customers' needs. They yearn to understand their customers better so that they can improve their products or create new ones that are actually needed. They invest in focus groups, surveys, trials and any number of other approaches to get second-hand input. Social platforms provide a direct connection between those who have spotted 'a gap in the market' and want to fill it and those who can manufacture something. Fiat Brazil unveiled the first crowdsourced concept car, the Mio, at the International Automobile Fair in São Paulo in 2010. Threadless Tees pays cash for designs that are sourced from its customers. My Starbucks Ideas has gathered over 100,000 ideas, many of which are now products like sugar-free syrups, the key chain card and tall reusable cold cups. Netflix started a competition in 2009 to find an algorithm that improved its prediction accuracy, and awarded a cool $1 million at a ceremony in New York to the winning team of seven innovators. One company, Innocentive, has been running an open innovation crowdsourcing platform for over a decade. The company, incubated by Eli Lilly, has access to more than 250,000 'solvers' who apply themselves to real business problems in the form of incentivised challenges. They have run more than 1,300 public and over a 1,000 internal challenges sourced by employee groups, alumni, even retirees.

Ahhha is a social ideation platform which has come up with ideas like foot pedal-operated toilet seats, lightbulbs that never burn out and clip-on 3D spectacles for myopic moviegoers. If the ideas are good enough, the community of designers, engineers and funders becomes involved. Those behind Ahhha remind us that genius is 1 per cent inspiration and 99 per cent perspiration – ratios that Fried would no doubt agree with, even if both are needed.

The Self-Organising Crowd

Decisions about innovation are one thing, but what about the millions of decisions that keep an organisation going in the same direction? What about the micro-decisions that make the difference between a well-orchestrated group and a disorganised mob? Is it possible for everyone to walk, even run, in the same direction without leadership? There are examples in nature of distributed governance. Ants have no leader and bees build hives, but no individual bee could.

One experiment conducted by Loren Carpenter, co-founder of animation studio Pixar, surmises that passengers may be able to fly their own plane. Carpenter is an expert in computer graphics, a researcher and inventor. In 1991, he conducted an experiment in human collective behaviour. The experiment, documented in Kevin Kelly's book *Out of Control*, took place in a crowded conference hall in Las Vegas. Carpenter first asked around 5,000 attendees at a computer graphics conference to divide into two groups and play a simple game of Pong. Then Carpenter moved on to a flight simulator. Each participant was connected to a network via a virtual joystick. Each of the co-pilots could move the plane's up/down and left/right controls, and a virtual jet aircraft responded to the average of the decisions of the participants. According to Kelly, co-founder of *Wired*, this was a ludicrous exercise in passengers collectively flying their own plane. The passengers, Kelly goes on to explain, got to vote for everything – not only where the group was headed, but when to trim the flaps. As the participants began to take their plane down for landing, the auditorium erupted into shouts of 'Green, green!' and 'More red!' The flight simulator provided delayed feedback from lever to effect, from the moment that the aileron was tapped to the point when the plan banked. This caused the pilots to become trapped in what Kelly calls 'oscillations of overcompensation'. The plane pitched to the left, and looked like it was going to hit the landing strip wing-first. The plane lurched wildly, and yet the crowd somehow pulled the plane up, aborted the landing and turned the plane around to try again. How they turned the plane around in that way is fascinating, because no one was in charge. Five thousand novices were able to fly a jet with almost no direction or co-ordination from above. Kelly argued that the delegates were doing what birds do – they flocked. Flocking behaviour in birds, like shoaling behaviour of fish, is a complex set of patterns arising out of simple rules followed by a large number of individuals without any central co-ordination. However, unlike birds unaware of their collective shape, size or alignment, the conferees were conscious of the whole. They were following their plane on an immense screen.

Shortly, this self-conscious flocking afforded the crowd the ability to perform a 360, to roll the plane on their first flight in a way that was almost graceful. The crowd rewarded themselves with a standing ovation.

Flocking is an emergent behaviour. It is not planned or choreographed. It arises from simple, instinctive rules, like not crowding a neighbour and moving towards the average heading of the group. It is no surprise that we can organise ourselves in this way. A brief walk along London's South Bank with hordes of other tourists is an exercise in how we self-organise – all reach destinations, individuals and groups, with surprisingly few bumps.

One business that is built on self-organisation is Semco, a Brazilian manufacturing conglomerate. The business, which manufactures over 2,000 products, including dishwashers, marine pumps and mixing equipment, is built around self-managed teams. CEO Ricardo Semler wanted to share decision making with the people doing the work and connect them to the customer. Semco employees, 'Associates', make both tactical and strategic decisions, including those that might relate to products or new plant locations. There are no receptionists and no personal assistants. Semco staff arrange their own appointments and draft their own correspondence. There are very few rules, too. Staff set their own working hours and pay. The Semco policy manual is a twenty-page booklet with cartoons and brief declarations. According to Semler, with few exceptions, rules and regulations only serve to 'divert attention from the company's objectives, provide a false sense of security for executives, create work for bean counters and teach men to stone dinosaurs and start fires with sticks'.

Crowds may need fewer rules and co-operate more naturally than we think. Semco's revenues are around $200 million a year, it employs around 3,000 people, and it has been visited by at least 150 of the Fortune 500 in an effort to understand just how it is done. Says Semler: 'I am often asked, "How do you control a system like this?" I answer, "I don't. I let the system work for itself."'

The Knowledgeable Crowd

Of all the conjectures made by James Surowiecki in his definitive book *The Wisdom of Crowds*, the most challenging is that in some situations groups can be smarter than the smartest person in them. This defies conventional wisdom. For example, I am an amateur investor. I regularly invest a small amount in the

UK stock market. As a stock dabbler, I can accept that the experts will usually do better than me. That's a given. However, I struggle with the notion that lots of dabblers can do better than the experts.

I pick individual stocks, not out of any misplaced faith in my own expertise, but because I enjoy the process of researching, selecting and then following a company – not just the share price, which inevitably plummets, but more generally. If I stopped enjoying losing money in this way, I do have alternatives. I could invest in a mutual fund. A mutual fund is collected from similarly small investors so that it is sufficiently large to afford the luxury of being managed by an expert. Professional fund managers pick the stocks for us. With all that buying power, the fund manager can also diversify across a wider spread of stocks, even invest in other markets like bonds to protect the fund from a wide-scale stock market downturn. Professional fund managers work for major financial services business like Investec, UBS and Fidelity. They have impeccable educational and professional credentials, and are supported by the very best information systems. When Surowiecki talks about the smartest person in the room, these are the guys he is referring to. I have one more alternative beyond the DIY or expert approaches. I could automatically select stocks representative of the market, based on one of the many indexes, such as the FTSE 100. This requires no intelligence, and by definition it is always going to follow rather than beat the market, so this doesn't sound like a great way of beating our fund managers, our experts. Except it is. In 2011, 67 per cent of fund managers under-performed against the market. In spite of all the advantages, the systems, the information, the professional credentials, almost 70 per cent of fund managers didn't beat their benchmark. Of course, financial markets have been through turbulent times, but this doesn't explain it. Even during the good times, the picture is the same. According to The Motley Fool, between 1964 and 1998, 80 per cent of funds under-performed the stock market as it was represented by the Standard & Poor 500 index. When it comes to the decision 'Which stock should I pick?', we have 50 years of evidence to prove that the small group of experts is consistently and definitively beaten by the group.

Surowiecki uses another stock market example: the reaction to the Space Shuttle Challenger disaster, to illustrate what is at play here and why crowdsourced decisions can be wise ones. In their paper 'The Stock Price Reaction to the Challenger Crash: Information Disclosure in an Efficient Market', Michael T. Maloney and J. Harold Mulherin provide evidence that the market reacted more wisely and more quickly than government or NASA experts to pinpoint the culpable corporation and punish its stock price.

On 28 January 1986, at 11:39 Eastern Standard Time, the tragic explosion occurred. An announcement was made on the Dow Jones news wire at 11:47. The stock market didn't pause to show its respects. Trading was vigorous in the four Shuttle firms: Rockwell International, the maker of the Shuttle and main engines, Lockheed, the manager of ground support, Martin Marietta, manufacturer of the external fuel tank, and Morton Thiokol, the maker of the solid-fuel booster rocket. It would prove to be months before there was an answer to the reasons for the crash. On the following day, the headlines in the *New York Times* asked 'How could it happen?', and suggested that there were 'no ideas yet to the cause'. Ultimately, President Reagan appointed a panel headed by the former Secretary of State, William Rogers, which concluded in June that the cause of the crash was the lack of resiliency at low temperatures in the seals of the Shuttle's booster rockets supplied by Morton Thiokol. Without knowing any of this on the day of the crash, the market appeared to have held Morton Thiokol accountable. Within 13 minutes of the news wire announcement, Lockheed fell by 5.05 per cent, Martin Marietta 2.83 per cent and Rockwell 6.12 per cent. Sell activity in Morton Thiokol was so high that trading was halted. By the end of the day, Lockheed fell 2.14 per cent, Martin Marietta by 3.25 per cent and Rockwell by 2.48 per cent, while Morton Thiokol fell by 11.86 per cent.

Out of the four suppliers, the crowd identified the culprit just hours after the disaster, while the Rogers Commission needed five more months. Maloney and Mulherin concluded that traders quickly pieced together 'private information' from multiple sources. This private information might be characterised as ambient knowledge – small fragments of information that had previously been thought of as insignificant. They might have included information on social interactions that were too expensive to capture but were, in the light of the disaster, invaluable, whatever effort was required to piece together recollections, opinions and conversations. The crowd had proved to be smart. Sufficiently motivated, it was able to pull together large volumes of ambient knowledge. In addition, the crowd fulfilled criteria that, according to Surowiecki, separate wise crowds from stupid mobs. It was diverse, independent, decentralised and efficiently aggregated. Members of the crowd had access to private ambient data. Their opinions are not determined by those around them, decisions were decentralised, and the stock market provides an efficient mechanism for converting private judgements into collective decisions.

The Co-ordinated Crowd

Involving more people in the decision process involves sharing information, collecting opinions and debating alternatives – all of which become exponentially more complex when you involve larger groups. The greater the number of participants, the slower and more difficult it is to orchestrate a decision, while fewer participants means increased speed and control. The cost of organising increases to a level exceeding the value of the improved decision. Or at least that used to be the case.

In his influential article 'The Nature of the Firm', Nobel Prize winner Ronald Coase explains why, if markets are efficient, they comprise firms, rather than consisting exclusively of individuals contracting with one another. The reason, Coase concludes, is that operating in a market requires transaction costs other than those for the goods or service. These include the cost of discovering which customers, partners and suppliers one wishes to deal with. Other transaction costs relate to information, bargaining and decisions. Coase's theory is that if transaction costs are low, the direct market of individuals is efficient. If transaction costs are higher, then an organisation is necessary. Coase's ceiling is the point at which adding one more person to an organisation creates more work than the individual can possibly contribute. Social tools lower the cost of organising. Clay Shirky, in his book *Here Comes Everybody*, argues that the cost of organising is close to zero. Shirky suggests there is a 'Coase floor'. This is why loosely connected groups can compile an encyclopaedia and build a computer operating system. Of course, both of these things have been achieved without any economic incentive, too, but that's been well covered by Shirky, Don Tapscott and Anthony D. Williams in their book *Wikinomics* and others. Instead, we are concerned with how loosely structured groups operate with minimal management inside an organisation.

Social platforms lower the cost of organising and remove many of the barriers to working together, like scheduling and the logistics involved in finding the right participants, forming, maintaining communications and establishing group processes. A collaborative culture that rejects hierarchy and works to reduce personality conflicts further removes barriers. Systematic support for the interactions around a decision means that group size and location are not constraining factors. Decisions can be challenged, challenges can be countered; discussions can take place without the need to be in the same time zone, let alone the same meeting room.

Conclusion

Thomas H. Davenport, author of *Analytics at Work* and holder of the President's Chair in Information Technology and Management at Babson College, Massachusetts attributes a growing number of disastrous private and public sector decisions, including investing in and securitising subprime mortgage loans, to the fact that decisions have become the 'prerogative of individuals'. In his article 'Make Better Decisions' for *Harvard Business Review*, Davenport argues that examples of poor corporate decisions, including the Time Warner acquisition of AOL and Yahoo! rejecting increasingly generous acquisition offers from Microsoft, are solo decisions. They are effectively failed heroic decisions.

Better decisions could be made by groups. They can be smarter. They can generate a diverse range of decision alternatives, guard against personal bias and introduce diversity. The combination of open, socially aligned organisations and social platforms remove many of the barriers that have previously prevented wider participation. Wider participation in the process means greater buy-in during execution. The result is that crowdsourced decision making is timely, smart, objective, balanced and aligned. It is decisions made and implemented by the crowd that are truly heroic.

12

Afterword

What technology is really about is better ways to evolve. That is what we call an 'infinite game.' ... A finite game is played to win, and an infinite game is played to keep playing.

Kevin Kelly

Those of you who have arrived at this point via the previous 11 chapters are living proof that in spite of living with information 'hyper-abundance', we are still capable of engaging in long-form argument. There are those, like Nicholas G. Carr, author of *The Shallows: How the Internet is Changing the Way We Think, Read and Remember*, who will be delighted that you have practised the ancient art of 'deep reading'. I stand right beside them as they shake your hands and thank you for joining us on this journey. I trust the trip has been worthwhile, without too many diversions or wrong turns. If for you there were, then please let me know. *Decision Sourcing* is not a destination, this is just a waypoint, and you can join us on Twitter, the blog or the website to share your views and help us to continue to make the map.

Along the way, we have asserted that businesses succeed, like we all do, by making good decisions. Interestingly, 'like we all do' has been a frequent diversion. Corporations, given rights and status as separate legal entities, ought to act more like people. They can be least human when mistakes are made, relying on posturing and positioning. When Electronic Arts received a Worst Company award from online consumer magazine *The Consumerist*, it responded with the statement: 'We're sure that British Petroleum, AIG, Philip Morris and Halliburton are all relieved they weren't nominated this year. We're going to continue making award-winning games and services played by more than 300 million people worldwide.'

If this is human, it is in a bad mood. The statement is at best dismissive, and at worst arrogant. We don't respond well to this. Human relationships survive the worst of mistakes, but through humility, not hubris. Few of us demand perfection of others, but we insist on authenticity. Companies shouting about being 'world-class' and 'best of breed' are mostly being ignored. Those of us with birth certificates rather than articles of incorporation are too busy actually communicating so that we can understand and help one another. These conversations are greatly aided by a new class of system: *the social app*. It means that people connect and groups form in a way that is not just easy, it is what Clay Shirky describes as 'ridiculously' easy. Companies have to take notice because well-organised groups now turn to each other rather than to them. We listen to one another while largely ignoring marketing brochures and the corporate website.

Impatience is one of the forces of the social revolution. Instead of waiting to be equipped with tablets, mobiles and social tools, we took the ones we used at home to work. There is sometimes some confusion because the word 'social' is commonly used to refer to activity outside work. However, the company is a clear example of a social group. It has the two critical elements: people and common purpose. Therefore, in this context 'social' also denotes a changing attitude in business. It signifies openness over opacity, authenticity over traditional (inauthentic) messaging, a human connection rather than an impersonal process.

Social inside and outside the organisation is putting pressure on inflexible processes and the systems that support them. It is also changing attitudes and behaviours. For example, social communication is completely open. Unlike meetings, phone calls and email, the dialogue is there for all to see – for ever. It demands honesty and congruence, living as if in an open-plan office and assuming that meetings and phone calls can and will be overheard. The presumption when composing emails is that they will be shared beyond those on the 'To' and 'Copy' lists. The ambition is to never be embarrassed or compromised by one's own words. Those who practise the approach know that this level of vigilance and circumspection requires a lifelong commitment. The reward, though, is a level of honesty that is liberating for those who live it, and deeper levels of trust from those around it.

Discourse that is captured in a social app is available for analysis so that those who choose to listen will get to know what their customers and staff really think. Those who are smart will not just listen, they will engage. The social enterprise, then, is equipped with tools that help to understand how people really connect, and it has little to do with the organisation chart which loses its relevance as soon as the induction training is completed. The enterprise social graph, like its Facebook equivalent, exposes how decisions are really made. A group forms for each decision, its constituents taking on roles that are not just about the provision of information. Decisions are infused with innovation and creative options. Opinions can be solicited and choices debated gracefully, so that when the decision is put into action, everyone is behind it. Those musing on how we can make the time for inclusive decisions should make a quick mental calculation on how much time is currently spent selling a decision made at the top of the organisation with little or no consultation

Listening isn't easy, though. It requires context, empathy and human understanding. Social listening attempts to do this, and at scale. Like Jim Carrey's character Bruce Nolen in *Bruce Almighty* when he is given God-like powers, it attempts to be omniscient – always listening, all conversations, all the time and at the same time. But the benefits are significant. We all like being listened to; we all yearn to be understood. Those who commit to it and get close to their customers and their teams as a result don't look back. Their efforts are rewarded with an engaged workforce and loyal customers.

Decision sourcing, then, is an approach and an attitude. The approach – using social apps for inclusive, networked decisions – is the outworking of an attitude towards people. One that listens and respects their views. One that deals with uncertainty not by layering on more process, but by letting go of control, learning to trust and distributing responsibility. It eschews the notion that a few know better, and embraces the reality that the crowd knows more. There is an old saying, 'Business is business,' which is often used to excuse the shoddy treatment of people in what is inevitably the short-term interest of the business. It is as if, somehow, we should all believe that business is not personal when it evidently is. We develop relationships with customers, we spend a third of each working day with our co-workers, we share successes, flinch at our failures and sometimes lose sleep over one or the other. The word 'company' has its roots in the Latin words *companio*, meaning 'companions', and *cum panis*, meaning 'with bread', both of which suggest that it could not be more personal. Business isn't business at all – it's profoundly human.

Appendix A:
The Decision Sourcing Framework

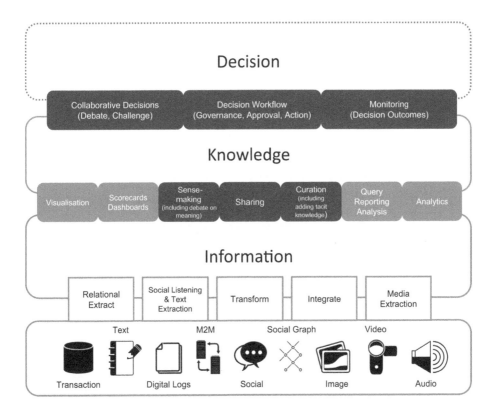

Figure A.1   The *Decision Sourcing* Organisational Decision Making
Framework

Appendix B:
Decision Anatomy

A Rational Model: The Pursuit of the Logic of Consequence

Decisions are a matter of:

1. **Alternatives** – What actions are possible?

2. **Expectations** – What future consequences might follow from each alternative?

3. **Preference** – How valuable to the decision maker are the consequences associated with each alternative?

4. **Decision rules** – How is a choice to be made among the alternatives in terms of the value of their consequences?[1]

The Seven Interaction Model

Decisions are a set of iterative interactions:

1. **Identify** – Monitor for problems, opportunities and exceptions.

2. **Frame** – Determine and agree the scope of the problem.

3. **Alternative** – Go through the creative process of developing alternatives.

---

1   James G. March, *A Primer on Decision Making.*

4.   **Criteria** – Agree the values on which the alternatives will be assessed.

5.   **Call** – Conduct a critical analysis of the alternatives and the selection of the preferred one.

6.   **Action** – Implement the decision.

7.   **Review** – Assess whether the decision was successful, learn lessons, reassess.[2]

---

2   Dale Roberts and Rooven Pakkiri, *Decision Sourcing.*

Appendix C:
Social Platforms

The technologies in the table below were reviewed, analysed and considered during the development of *Decision Sourcing*. This summary is not intended to be exhaustive, an endorsement of any specific product nor an indication that those missing from the analysis are in any way inferior. Rather, it demonstrates two categories of software converging and a third emerging, all into a new collaborative decision making (CDM) classification.

Other social technologies were researched in the interest of validating emerging trends, including Producteev, Badgeville, Bunchball, Kudos, BranchOut, Socialtext, Sprout, Klout, Kred, PeerIndex, Clearvale, Idiom, Auguri, Sparqlight, Salesforce Rypple, Igloo, Spigit, Powernoodle, Clarabridge, Social Mention, Artesian Solutions, FirstRain, Radian 6, Bazaarvoice, SAS and many others in a rapidly growing and changing arena.

For those businesses looking to begin or further their collaborative decision making journey, the authors would recommend a selection process based on your specific requirements and your current level of social adoption and maturity.

Table C.1   Collaborative decision making tools

Platform	Type	Graph (social only)	CDM role
Facebook	Social	Friends	Authentic source of consumer social intelligence
Twitter	Social	Lifestyle and professional	Authentic source of consumer and professional social intelligence
LinkedIn	Social	Professional	Authentic source of professional social intelligence
Yammer	Social	Enterprise	Enterprise collaborative platform
IBM Connections	Social	Enterprise	Enterprise collaborative platform, integration with IBM Cognos BI
Salesforce Chatter	Social	Enterprise	Enterprise collaborative platform
OpenText	Social	Enterprise	Enterprise collaborative platform
Saba	Social	Enterprise	Collaborative platform, origins in learning management
Jive	Social	Enterprise	Enterprise collaborative platform
Microsoft Sharepoint	Social	Enterprise	Platform on which CDM applications can be built
VMware Socialcast	Social	Enterprise	Enterprise collaborative platform
Citrix Podio	Social	Enterprise	Enterprise collaborative platform
SAP Streamwork	Decision making		Collaborative decision making platform
Decision Lens	Decision making		Collaborative decision making platform
Lyzasoft	Hyrbid		Collaborative decision making tied to BI
IBM Cognos BI	Analytics		Analytics integration with IBM Connections
SAP Business Objects	Analytics		Analytics integration with SAP Streamwork
Panorama Necto	Analytics		Collaboration around BI content
Qliktech Qlikview	Analytics		Collaboration around BI content
Tibco Spotfire	Analytics		Collaboration around BI content and integration with Tibco Tibbr

References

Ackoff, R.L. 'From Data to Wisdom'. *Journal of Applied Systems Analysis* 16 (1989): 3–9.

Adams, Paul. 'The Real Life Social Network V2'. slideshare, 1 July 2010. Accessed 4 June 2012. http://www.slideshare.net/padday/the-real-life-social-network-v2.

AHHHA, n.d. Accessed 5 June 2012. http://ahhha.com/.

Allen, David. *Getting Things Done: How to Achieve Stress-free Productivity*. New York: Viking, 2001.

Allen, Tom J. *Managing the Flow of Technology*. Cambridge, MA: MIT, 1978.

Andersen, Erika. *Being Strategic: Plan for Success; Out-think Your Competitors; Stay Ahead of Change*. New York: St. Martin's Press, 2009.

Andersen, Erika. *Growing Great Employees: Turning Ordinary People into Extraordinary Performers*. New York: Penguin, 2006.

Andersen, Erika. 'Why Top Talent Leaves: Top 10 Reasons Boiled Down to 1'. *Forbes*, 18 January 2012. Accessed 4 June 2012. http://www.forbes.com/sites/erikaandersen/2012/01/18/why-top-talent-leaves-top-10-reasons-boiled-down-to-1/.

Andrews, David. *The IRG Solution: Hierarchical Incompetence and How to Overcome It*. London: Souvenir, 1984.

Angell, David, Peter Casey, David Lee, Glen Charles, and Les Charles. 'Frasier'. *Frasier*. Paramount. 1993–2004.

Anon. 'Big Data: The Next Frontier for Innovation, Competition, and Productivity'. McKinsey Global Institute, McKinsey&Company, May 2011. Accessed 20 June 2012. http://www.mckinsey.com/Insights/MGI/Research/technology_and_Innovation/Big_data_The_next_frontier_for_innovation.

Anon. 'Biography: Howard Schultz, Starbucks'. myprimetime, n.d. Accessed 5 June 2012. http://www.myprimetime.com/work/ge/schultzbio/.

Anon. 'Customer Experience Can Generate $100s of Millions in Revenues, According to Groundbreaking Research from Temkin Group Research'. PR Newswire, 28 March 2012. Accessed 4 June 2012. http://www.prnewswire.com/

news-releases/customer-experience-can-generate-100s-of-millions-in-revenues-according-to-groundbreaking-research-from-temkin-group-research-144610935.html.

Anon. 'Decision-making in Organizations'. Orgnet.com, n.d. Accessed 4 June 2012. http://www.orgnet.com/decisions.html.

Anon. 'DMA Releases 2010 Response Rate Trend Report'. Direct Marketing Association, 15 June 2010. Accessed 4 June 2012. http://www.the-dma.org/cgi/dispannouncements?article=1451.

Anon. 'From Social Media to Social CRM: A Two-part Series'. IBM, February 2011. Accessed 4 June 2012. http://www-935.ibm.com/services/us/gbs/thoughtleadership/ibv-social-crm-whitepaper.html.

Anon. 'GeoPatterns – Mood of the Nation'. University of Bristol, n.d. Accessed 5 June 2012. http://geopatterns.enm.bris.ac.uk/mood/.

Anon. 'Glossary of Sensemaking Terms'. PARC, n.d. Accessed 5 June 2012. http://www2.parc.com/istl/groups/hdi/sensemaking/glossary.htm.

Anon. *How Social Technologies Drive Business Success*. Google and Millward Brown, 2012.

Anon. 'In Focus: e-diplomacy'. Diplo, n.d. Accessed 4 June 2012. http://www.diplomacy.edu/e-diplomacy.

Anon. 'Native American Legends'. First People, n.d. Accessed 4 June 2012. http://www.firstpeople.us/FP-Html-Legends/TraditionalTalkingStick-Unknown.html.

Anon. 'Oscar Senti-meter'. The Envelope, *Los Angeles Times*, 2 March 2012. Accessed 4 June 2012. http://graphics.latimes.com/senti-meter/.

Anon. 'Presenting: The Top 25 Social CIOs in the Fortune 250'. Harmon.ie, May 2012. Accessed 5 June 2012. http://harmon.ie/blog/04-04-2012.

Anon. 'Renowned Italian Football Club Turns to CA's CleverPath to Achieve New Conditioning and Injury-reduction Goals'. PR Newswire, 26 March 2010. Accessed 5 June 2012. http://www.prnewswire.com/news-releases/renowned-italian-football-club-turns-to-cas-cleverpath-to-achieve-new-conditioning-and-injury-reduction-goals-76621252.html.

Anon. 'Social Network Analysis, A Brief Introduction'. Orgnet.com, n.d. Accessed 4 June 2012. http://www.orgnet.com/sna.html.

Anon. 'Study Analyzes Twitter as News Source during Arab Spring'. Phys.Org, 20 March 2012. Accessed 4 June 2012. http://phys.org/news/2012-03-twitter-news-source-arab.html.

Anon. 'The Art of Stillspotting: Questions for the Guggenheim's David Van Der Leer'. Brooklyn Based, 30 May 2011. Accessed 5 June 2012. http://brooklynbased.net/blog/2011/05/the-art-of-stillspotting-questions-for-the-guggenheim%E2%80%99s-david-van-der-leer/.

Anon. 'The Cases of Daniel McCallum and Gustavus Swift'. Williamette University, n.d. Accessed 4 June 2012. http://www.willamette.edu/~fthompso/MgmtCon/McCallum.htm.

Anon. 'The History of CRM – Evolving beyond the Customer Database'. CRMSoftwareGuide, January 2008. Accessed 4 June 2012. http://www.crm-software-guide.com/history-of-crm.htm.

Anon. 'TikTok'. LunaTik, n.d. Accessed 4 June 2012. https://www.lunatik.com/products.

Anon. 'Why Middle Managers May be the Most Important People in Your Company'. Knowledge@Wharton, 25 May 2011. Accessed 4 June 2012. http://knowledge.wharton.upenn.edu/article.cfm?articleid=2783.

Ariely, Dan. Predictably Irrational: The Hidden Forces that Shape Our Decisions. New York: HarperCollins, 2008.

Arthur, Charles. 'What is the 1% Rule?', The Guardian, 20 July 2006. Accessed 4 June 2012. http://www.guardian.co.uk/technology/2006/jul/20/guardianweeklytechnologysection2.

Ashkenas, Ronald N. 'Your Career Needs to be Horizontal'. HBR Blog Network, Harvard Business Review, 27 March 2012. Accessed 6 June 2012. http://blogs.hbr.org/ashkenas/2012/03/your-career-needs-to-be-horizo.html.

Ayers, Michael D. 'Domino's Says No to Fake Food Styling'. Slashfood, 8 July 2010. Accessed 4 June 2012. http://www.slashfood.com/2010/07/08/dominos-says-no-to-fake-food-styling/.

Bakan, Joel. The Corporation: The Pathological Pursuit of Profit and Power. New York: The Free Press, 2004.

Baker, Loren. 'Yahoo Reorganization Focuses on Audiences, Advertisers & Publishers'. Search Engine Journal, 6 December 2006. Accessed 4 June 2012. http://www.searchenginejournal.com/yahoo-reorganization-focuses-on-audiences-advertisers-publishers/4073/.

Barabási, Albert-László. Linked: The New Science of Networks. Cambridge, MA: Perseus Publishing.

Barkham, Patrick. 'What is the Knowledge Economy?' The Guardian, 16 July 2008. Accessed 3 June 2012. http://www.guardian.co.uk/business/2008/jul/17/economics.economicgrowth.

Barnett, Emma. 'Facebook Cuts Six Degrees of Separation to Four'. The Telegraph, 22 November 2011. Accessed 4 June 2012. http://www.telegraph.co.uk/technology/facebook/8906693/Facebook-cuts-six-degrees-of-separation-to-four.html.

Bevins, Timothy, and Naumi Haque. 'Data Enabled Collaborative Decision-Making: A Guide for Next Generation Enterprise Decision Processes'. Moxie

Insight, 11 January 2011. Accessed 22 January 2013. http://moxieinsight.com/resourcesandevents/reports/data-enabled-collaborative-decision-making/.

Blenko, Marcia W., Michael C. Mankins and Paul Rogers. 'The Decision-driven Organization'. *Harvard Business Review*, 1 June 2010. Accessed 4 June 2012. http://hbr.org/product/the-decision-driven-organization/an/R1006B-PDF-ENG.

Bloxham, Andy. 'Twitter Becomes Latest Tool for Hedge Fund Managers'. *The Telegraph*, 11 September 2011.

Bodell, Lisa. '5 Ways Process is Killing Your Productivity'. *Fast Company*, 15 May 2012. Accessed 4 June 2012. http://www.fastcompany.com/1837301/5-ways-process-kills-productivity.

Bodell, Lisa. *Kill the Company: End the Status Quo, Start an Innovation Revolution.* Brookline, MA: Bibliomotion, 2012.

Bollen, Johan, Huina Mao, and Xiaojun Zeng. 'Twitter Mood Predicts the Stock Market'. *Journal of Computational Science* 2:1 (2011): 1–8.

Bowling, Drew. 'The Entertainment Industry is Actually Booming, So … Why SOPA?' WebProNews, 30 January 2007. Accessed 5 June 2012. http://www.webpronews.com/the-entertainment-industry-is-actually-booming-so%E2%80%A6-why-sopa-2012-01.

Breen, Bill. 'What's Your Intuition?' *Fast Company*, 31 August 2000. Accessed 4 June 2012. http://www.fastcompany.com/magazine/38/klein.html.

Bruce Almighty. Perf. Jim Carrey. Universal Studios, 2003. Film.

Brustein, Joshua. 'Why Innovation Doffs an Old Hat'. *The New York Times*, 13 February 2011. Accessed 5 June 2012. http://www.nytimes.com/2011/02/13/weekinreview/13brustein.html?_r=3.

Bryant, Lee. 'The Social Business Index is Open'. *Headshift*, 13 September 2011. Accessed 4 June 2012. http://www.headshift.com/our-blog/2011/09/13/the-social-business-index-is-open/.

Buckman, Rebecca. 'The Yahoo! Reorg Begins'. *Forbes*, 26 February 2009. Accessed 4 June 2012. http://www.forbes.com/2009/02/26/yahoo-carol-bartz-technology-internet_yahoo.html.

Byl, Bart. 'What a Cab Driver Can Teach You About Social Media'. Sales Force Marketing Cloud, 11 April 2012. Accessed 4 June 2012. http://www.radian6.com/blog/2012/04/what-a-cab-driver-can-teach-you-about-social-media/.

Cadsby, Ted. 'Why Being Certain Means Being Wrong'. HBR Blog Network, *Harvard Business Review*, 25 July 2011. Accessed 4 June 2012. http://blogs.hbr.org/cs/2011/07/why_being_certain_means_being.html.

Cantril, Hadley and Charles Heath Bumstead. *Reflections on the Human Venture.* New York: New York University Press, 1960.

Capellá, Jaime, Andrew Horne and Shvetank Shah. 'Good Data Won't Guarantee Good Decisions'. *Harvard Business Review*, April 2012. Accessed 5 June 2012. http://hbr.org/2012/04/good-data-wont-guarantee-good-decisions/ar/1.

Capitalizing on Complexity: Insights from the 2010 IBM Global CEO Study. Report. IBM, 2010.

Carlin, Peter. 'How to Make a Decision Like a Tribe'. *Fast Company*, 31 October 1995. Accessed 5 June 2012. http://www.fastcompany.com/magazine/01/rainbow.html.

Carlson, Nicholas. 'The Real History Of Twitter'. *Business Insider*, 13 April 2011. Accessed 5 June 2012. http://articles.businessinsider.com/2011-04-13/tech/29957143_1_jack-dorsey-twitter-podcasting.

Carr, Nicholas G. *The Shallows: How the Internet is Changing the Way We Think, Read and Remember*. London: Atlantic Books, 2010.

Chandler, Alfred. *The Visible Hand: Managerial Revolution in American Business*. Cambridge, MA: Harvard University Press, 1977.

Coase, Ronald. 'The Nature of the Firm'. *Economica* 4:16 (November 1937): 386–405.

Cohen, Michael D., James G. March and Johan P. Olsen. 'A Garbage Can Model of Organizational Choice'. *Administrative Science Quarterly* (1972): 1–25, March 1972. Accessed 12 December 2012. http://links.jstor.org/sici?sici=0001-8392%28197203%2917%3A1%3C1%3AAGCMOO%3E2.0.CO%3B2-9.

Collins, Jim. *Good to Great: Why Some Companies Make the Leap … and Others Don't*. London: Random House, 2001.

Collins, Michael P. 'Trash Your Employee Handbook'. *Manufacturing.Net*, 11 October 2011. Accessed 5 June 2012. http://www.manufacturing.net/articles/2011/11/trash-your-employee-handbook.

Cook, Niall. *Enterprise 2.0: How Social Software Will Change the Future of Work*. Aldershot: Gower, 2008.

Corporate Executive Board. 'Overcoming the Insight Deficit: Getting from Big Data to Big Judgment'. CEB Advisory, 2012. Accessed 22 January 2013. http://www.executiveboard.com/exbd/information-technology/insight-deficit/index.page.

Crawley, Jim and Nick Tatchell. 'Towers Perrin Global Workforce Study'. *The Economist*, 13 November 2007. Accessed 5 June 2012. http://viewswire.eiu.com/index.asp?layout=EBArticleVW3.

Cree, Richard. 'Sir Terry Leahy, CEO, Tesco'. *Director*, February 2011. Accessed 5 June 2012. http://www.director.co.uk/magazine/2011/2_Feb/terry-leahy_64_06.html.

Cross, Robert L. and Andrew Parker. *The Hidden Power of Social Networks: Understanding How Work Really Gets Done in Organizations*. Boston, MA: Harvard Business School, 2004.

Cross, Robert L., Andrew Parker and Lisa Sasson. *Networks in the Knowledge Economy*. New York: Oxford University Press, 2003.

Davenport, Thomas H. *Analytics at Work: Smarter Decisions, Better Results*. Boston, MA: Harvard Business School.

Davenport, Thomas H. 'Make Better Decisions'. *Harvard Business Review*, November 2009. Accessed 5 June 2012. http://hbr.org/2009/11/make-better-decisions/ar/.

Davenport, Thomas H. and Jeanne G. Harris. *Competing on Analytics: The New Science of Winning*. Boston, MA: Harvard Business School, 2007.

de Botton, Alain. *The Pleasures and Sorrows of Work*. New York: Random House, 2010.

Dervin, Brenda, 'Brenda Dervin – Info'. Facebook, n.d. Accessed 5 June 2012. https://www.facebook.com/pages/Brenda-Dervin/133536936686481?sk=info.

Devlin, Barry. 'Collaborative BI – What Women and Men Want'. Smart Data Collective, 27 March 2012. Accessed 4 June 2012. http://smartdatacollective. com/barry-devlin/48779/collaborative-bi-what-women-and-men-want.

Devlin, Barry. 'Seven Steps to Rejuvenating Your Strategic BI'. TDWI – The Data Warehousing Institute, n.d. Accessed 4 June 2012. http://tdwi.org/ webcasts/2011/05/seven-steps.aspx?tc=page0.

Dijoux, Cecil. 'Enterprise 2.0: Leveraging Collaboration Platforms to Foster Knowledge, Innovation and Productivity'. slideshare, 14 October 2009. Accessed 4 June 2012. http://www.slideshare.net/ceciiil/blah-blah-2219353.

Drucker, Peter F. *Management Challenges for the 21st Century*. New York: HarperCollins, 1999.

Drucker, Peter F. *Management: Tasks, Responsibilities, Practices*. New York: Harper & Row, 1973.

Elgan, Mike. 'Why Apple Has Already Pwned the Gaming Market'. Cult of Mac, n.d. Accessed 5 June 2012. http://www.cultofmac.com/162144/why-apple-has-already-pwned-the-gaming-market/.

Etlinger, Susan. 'A Framework for Social Analytics'. slideshare, 10 August 2011. Accessed 4 June 2012. http://www.slideshare.net/setlinger/altimeter-social-analytics081011final.

Ewuvideo. 'Eastern Spotlight: Brenda Dervin', n.d. YouTube, 1 March 2011. Accessed 5 June 2012. http://www.youtube.com/watch?v=foyH6eoIseQ.

Filmer, Deon. 'Deon Filmer'. World Bank Blogs, April 2010. Accessed 4 June 2012. https://blogs.worldbank.org/education/team/deon-filmer.

Finkelstein, Sydney. *Why Smart Executives Fail: And What You Can Learn from Their Mistakes*. London: Penguin, 2003.

Finkelstein, Sydney, Jo Whitehead and Andrew Campbell. *Think Again: Why Good Leaders Make Bad Decisions and How to Keep It from Happening to You*. Boston, MA: Harvard Business School, 2008.

Finley, Klint. 'Business Analytics Predictions from Gartner and Forrester'. ReadWrite Enterprise, 6 January 2011. Accessed 4 June 2012. http://www. readwriteweb.com/enterprise/2011/01/business-analytics-predictions.php.

Fisk, Donald M. 'American Labor in the 20th Century'. US Bureau of Labor Statistics, 30 January 2003. Accessed 4 June 2012. http://www.bls.gov/opub/ cwc/cm20030124ar02p1.htm.

Fitzpatrick, Brad. 'Thoughts on the Social Graph'. bradfitz.com, 17 August 2007. Accessed 4 June 2012. http://bradfitz.com/social-graph-problem/.

Fleck, Chris. '30 Years Later the PC Revolution is Here Again'. The Citrix Blog, 12 August 2011. Accessed 4 June 2012. http://blogs.citrix.com/2011/08/12/30-years-later-the-pc-revolution-is-here-again/.

Forrester Research. 'US Telecommuting Forecast, 2009 To 2016'. 11 March 2009. Accessed 22 January 2013. http://www.forrester.com/US+Telecommuting+F orecast+2009+To+2016/fulltext/-/E-RES46635?objectid=RES46635.

Fried, Jason and David Heinemeier Hansson. *ReWork: Change the Way You Work Forever*. London: Vermilion, 2010.

Frommer, Dan. 'Yahoo Reorg is On: New Jobs for Ash Patel, Hilary Schneider (YHOO)'. *Business Insider*, 26 June 2008. Accessed 4 June 2012. http://articles. businessinsider.com/2008-06-26/tech/30099811_1_audience-products-division-yahoo-s-global-prabhakar-raghavan.

Gallagher, Deb. 'The Decline of the HPPO (Highest Paid Person's Opinion)'. *MIT Sloan Management Review*, 4 January 2012. Accessed 4 June 2012. http:// sloanreview.mit.edu/improvisations/2012/04/01/the-decline-of-the-hppo-highest-paid-persons-opinion/.

Garbuio, Massimo, Dan Lovallo and Patrick Viguerie. 'How Companies Make Good Decisions'. *McKinsey Quarterly* (2009). Accessed 12 December 2012. http://www.washburn.edu/faculty/rweigand/McKinsey/McKinsey-How-Companies-Make-Good-Decisions.pdf.

Garvin, David A. and Michael A. Roberto. 'What You Don't Know About Making Decisions – HBS Working Knowledge'. Harvard Business School, 15 October 2001. Accessed 6 June 2012. http://hbswk.hbs.edu/item/2544.html.

Garvin, David A. 'Executive Decision Making at General Motors (TN)'. Harvard Business School Case 305-026, December 2004.

Gaudin, Sharon. 'Yahoo Prepping Reorg and Massive Layoffs, Report Says'. Computerworld, 5 March 2012. Accessed 4 June 2012. http://www. computerworld.com/s/article/9224888/Yahoo_prepping_reorg_and_ massive_layoffs_report_says.

Gebauer, Julie. 'Key Findings: An Interview with Julie Gebauer on Towers Perrin's Just Released Global Workforce Study, Part 2'. Towers Watson, n.d. Accessed 5 June 2012. http://www.towersperrin.com/tp/showhtml. jsp?url=global/publications/gws/key-findings_2.htm.

Gillet, Frank. 'Employees Use Multiple Gadgets For Work—And Choose Much Of The Tech Themselves'. 22 February 2012. Accessed 3 January 2013. http://blogs.forrester.com/frank_gillett/12-02-22-employees_use_multiple_gadgets_for_work_and_choose_much_of_the_tech_themselves.

Giuliani, Rudy. 'The Rudy Record: Crime Reduction'. Giuliani Blog, 27 November. 2006. Accessed 5 June 2012. http://giulianiblog.blogspot.co.uk/2006/11/rudy-record-crime-reduction.html.

Gladwell, Malcolm. *Blink: The Power of Thinking Without Thinking*. London: Penguin, 2005.

Gray, Dave. 'A Business within the Business'. Dachis Group, 28 November 2011. Accessed 5 June 2012. http://www.dachisgroup.com/2011/11/a-business-within-the-business/.

Gray, Louis. 'Activity Streams Aim to be DNA of the Future Web'. Louisgray.com, 13 March 2010. Accessed 5 June 2012. http://blog.louisgray.com/2010/03/activitystreams-aim-to-be-dna-of-future.html.

Grimes, Seth. 'Text Analytics for Dummies 2010'. slideshare, 25 May 2010. Accessed 4 June 2012. http://www.slideshare.net/SethGrimes/text-analytics-for-dummies-2010.

Grimes, Seth. 'Text Analytics Overview, 2011'. slideshare, 18 May 2011. Accessed 4 June 2012. http://www.slideshare.net/SethGrimes/text-analytics-overview-2011.

Grow, Brian and Brian Hindo. 'Six Sigma: So Yesterday?' *Bloomberg Business Week*, 11 June 2007. Accessed 4 June 2012. http://www.businessweek.com/magazine/content/07_24/b4038409.htm.

Haksi, Sandy. 'Black Out Speak Out'. The Corporation.com Blog, 4 June 2004. Accessed 12 December 2012. http://www.thecorporation.com/blog.cfm?view=BLOG_POST&blog_id=463.

Hamel, Gary. 'Management's Dirty Little Secret'. Gary Hamel's Management 2.0, *The Wall Street Journal*, 16 December 2009. Accessed 5 June 2012. http://blogs.wsj.com/management/2009/12/16/management%E2%80%99s-dirty-little-secret/.

Hamel, Gary. 'Moon Shots for Management'. *Harvard Business Review*, February 2009. Accessed 5 June 2012. http://hbr.org/2009/02/moon-shots-for-management/ar/1.

Hamel, Gary. *What Matters Now: How to Win in a World of Relentless Change, Ferocious Competition, and Unstoppable Innovation*. San Francisco, CA: Jossey-Bass, 2012.

Happe, Rachel. 'Decision Making in a Networked World'. The Social Organization, 26 July 2011. Accessed 4 June 2012. http://www.thesocialorganization. com/2011/07/decision-making-in-a-networked-world.html.

Harquail, C.V. 'Networks and the Myth that Flatter Organizations are Better'. Authentic Organizations, 24 May 2012. Accessed 4 June 2012. http:// authenticorganizations.com/harquail/2010/01/15/networks-and-the-myth-that-flatter-organizations-are-better/.

Harris, Derrick. 'How Social Media is Making Polling Obsolete'. GigaOM, 10 February 2012. Accessed 4 June 2012. http://gigaom.com/cloud/how-social-media-is-making-polling-obsolete/.

Heineman, Jr, Ben W. 'Steve Jobs and the Purpose of the Corporation'. HBR Blog Network, *Harvard Business Review*, 12 October 2011. Accessed 5 June 2012. http://blogs.hbr.org/cs/2011/10/steve_jobs_and_the_purpose_of.html.

Hinchcliffe, Dion. 'Social Business Moves to Workflow, Manufacturing, and Money'. Dachis Group, 27 September 2011. Accessed 4 June 2012. http:// www.dachisgroup.com/2011/09/social-business-moves-to-workflow-manufacturing-and-money/.

Huberman, Bernardo A. and Sitaram Asur. 'Predicting the Future with Social Media'. slideshare, March 2010. Accessed 4 June 2012. http://www.slideshare. net/mobile/napo/predicting-the-future-with-social-media-3799074.

Huleatt, Sam. 'The Rise of the Social Gesture'. Leveraging Ideas, 4 May 2010. Accessed 5 June 2012. http://www.leveragingideas.com/2010/05/04/the-rise-of-the-social-gesture/.

Husband, Jon. 'Wirearchy – What is Wirearchy?' Wirearchy, n.d. Accessed 4 June 2012. http://www.wirearchy.com/what-is-wirearchy/.

Huy, Quy Nguyen. 'In Praise of Middle Managers'. *Harvard Business Review*, September 2001. Accessed 4 June 2012. http://hbr.org/2001/09/in-praise-of-middle-managers/ar/1.

IBM. *Leading Through Connections: Insights from the IBM Global CEO Study*. Portsmouth: IBM, 2012. Accessed 12 December 2012. http://www-935.ibm. com/services/us/en/c-suite/ceostudy2012/.

Iskold, Alex. 'Social Graph: Concepts and Issues'. ReadWrite, 11 September 2007. Accessed 4 June 2012. http://www.readwriteweb.com/archives/social_ graph_concepts_and_issues.php.

Jarvis, Jeff. 'Ambient Intimacy'. BuzzMachine, 6 May 2008. Accessed 4 June 2012. http://buzzmachine.com/2008/05/06/ambient-intimacy/.

Jarvis, Jeff. 'Death of the Curator. Long Live the Curator'. BuzzMachine, 23 April 2009. Accessed 5 June 2012. http://buzzmachine.com/2009/04/23/death-of-the-curator-long-live-the-curator/.

Jarvis, Jeff. *Public Parts: How Sharing in the Digital Age Improves the Way We Work and Live*. New York: Simon & Schuster, 2011.

Jarvis, Jeff. *What Would Google Do? Reverse-engineering the Fastest Growing Company in the History of the World*. New York: Collins, 2009.

Jose, San. 'Social Network Participation Increasingly Affects Executive Decision Making, According to 2nd Annual New Symbiosis of Professional Networks Study'. PRWeb, 17 March 2011. Accessed 4 June 2012. http://www.prweb.com/releases/sncr/symbiosis_study/prweb5169454.htm.

Kadushin, Charles. *Understanding Social Networks: Theories, Concepts, and Findings*. Oxford: Oxford University Press, 2012.

Kamber, Micheline and Jiawei Han. 'Section 10.1. Mining Text and Web Data'. slideshare, 5 October 2010. Accessed 4 June 2012. http://www.slideshare.net/mobile/Tommy96/section-101-mining-text-and-web-data.

Kaplan, Robert S. and David P. Norton. *Alignment: Using the Balanced Scorecard to Create Corporate Synergies*. Boston, MA: Harvard Business School, 2006.

Keller, Monica. 'Activity Stream'. Prezi, 3 November 2009. Accessed 5 June 2012. http://prezi.com/yxvtypx-aani/activity-stream/.

Kelley, Braden. Braden Kelley Blog. Innovation Excellence, n.d. Accessed 5 June 2012. http://www.innovationexcellence.com/blog/author/braden-kelley/.

Kelly, Kevin. *Out of Control: The New Biology of Machines, Social Systems, and the Economic World*. Reading, MA: Addison-Wesley, 1995.

Kirkpatrick, David. 'Fast Forward: The World's Most Modern Management is in India'. CNNMoney, 14 April 2006. Accessed 5 June 2012. http://money.cnn.com/2006/04/13/magazines/fortune/fastforward_fortune/index.htm.

Kober, J. Jeff. 'Disney Service Basics'. Mouse Planet, 29 November 2007. Accessed 4 June 2012. http://www.mouseplanet.com/6978/Disney_Service_Basics.

Kober, J. Jeff. *The Wonderful World of Customer Service at Disney*. Orlando, FL: Performance Journeys, 2009.

Kobielus, James. 'Predictions for Business Analytics in 2011'. *InformationWeek Software*, 6 January 2011. Accessed 4 June 2012. http://www.informationweek.com/software/business-intelligence/predictions-for-business-analytics-in-20/229000253.

LaFemina, Diana. 'How Do We Know What We Know? Tacit Knowledge Defined'. Serendip, 2002. Accessed 4 June 2012. http://serendip.brynmawr.edu/biology/b103/f02/web2/dlafemina.html.

Langreth, Robert. 'Bristol-Myers CEO Gets 27% Pay Increase After Cancer Drug Sales Start Fast'. *Bloomberg*, 12 March 2012. Accessed 4 June 2012. http://www.bloomberg.com/news/2012-03-12/bristol-myers-ceo-gets-27-pay-increase-after-cancer-drug-sales-start-fast.html.

Leonard, Tom. 'Transcript Reveals Calm Manner of Hudson River Plane Crash Pilot'. *The Telegraph*, 5 February 2009. Accessed 4 June 2012. http://www.telegraph.co.uk/news/worldnews/northamerica/usa/4527418/Transcript-reveals-calm-manner-of-Hudson-River-plane-crash-pilot.html.

Lepofsky, Alan. 'Social Analytics – Practical Use Cases At Work'. slideshare, February 2012. Accessed 4 June 2012. http://www.slideshare.net/alanlepo/social-analytics-practical-use-cases-at-work.

Levitt, Steven D. and Stephen J. Dubner. *Freakonomics: A Rogue Economist Explores the Hidden Side of Everything*. New York: William Morrow, 2005.

Li, Charlene. 'Making the Business Case for Enterprise Social Networks'. Altimeter, 22 February 2009. Accessed 4 June 2012. http://www.altimetergroup.com/research/reports/making-the-business-case-for-enterprise-social-networks.

Locke, Chris, Doc Searls, David Weinberger and Rick Levine. 'people of earth...'. The Cluetrain Manifesto, April 1999. Accessed 4 June 2012. http://www.cluetrain.com/.

Locke, Chris, Doc Searls, David Weinberger and Rick Levine. *The Cluetrain Manifesto*. London: FT.com, 2000.

Maloney, Michael T. and J. Harold Mulherin. 'The Stock Price Reaction to the Challenger Crash: Information Disclosure in an Efficient Market'. Social Science Research Network, 7 December 1998. Accessed 5 June 2012. http://papers.ssrn.com/sol3/papers.cfm?abstract_id=141971.

Marca, Paul, J. Eric Bickel, Carl Spetzler and Hannah Winter. *Decision Quality: The Art and Science of Good Decision-making*. Stanford Strategic Decision and Risk Management Certificate Program, 10 November 2011.

March, James G. *A Primer on Decision Making: How Decisions Happen*. New York: The Free Press, 1994.

Maria. 'Your Community's Hidden Treasure is Lurking Right Over There'. Yammer The Blog, 20 June 2011. Accessed 4 June 2012. http://blog.yammer.com/blog/2011/07/your-community-hidden-treasure-lurking.html.

Marks, Oliver. '"The Purpose of a Business is to Create a Customer" – Peter Drucker Centenary'. ZDNet, 16 November 2009. Accessed 5 June 2012. http://www.zdnet.com/blog/collaboration/the-purpose-of-a-business-is-to-create-a-customer-peter-drucker-centenary/1049.

Matar, Hisham. 'Ways With Words: Role of Twitter and Facebook in Arab Spring Uprising "Overstated", Says Hisham Matar'. *The Telegraph*, 11 July 2011. Accessed 12 December 2012. http://www.telegraph.co.uk/culture/books/ways-with-words/8629294/Ways-With-Words-role-of-Twitter-and-Facebook-in-Arab-Spring-uprising-overstated-says-Hisham-Matar.html.

McCreary, Dan. 'Entity Extraction and the Semantic Web'. semanticweb.com, 12 January 2009. Accessed 4 June 2012. http://semanticweb.com/entity-extraction-and-the-semantic-web_b10675.

McDonald, Dennis D. 'How to Relate Kaplan and Norton's "Alignment" Process to Enterprise Web 2.0'. Dennis D. McDonald's Web Site, 28 April 2006. Accessed 5 June 2012. http://www.ddmcd.com/managing-technology/how-to-relate-kaplan-and-nortons-alignment-process-to-enterp.html.

McKinsey & Co. 'Distortions and Deceptions in Strategic Decisions'. CFO, 16 January 2006. Accessed 4 June 2012. http://www.cfo.com/article.cfm/5380604.

Messina, Chris. 'Activity Streams, Socialism, & the Future of Open Source'. slideshare, 1 June 2010. Accessed 5 June 2012. http://www.slideshare.net/factoryjoe/activity-streams-socialism-the-future-of-open-source.

Mohr, Elizabeth, Matthew Guthridge and Martin Dewhurst. 'Motivating People: Getting beyond Money'. McKinsey Quarterly, November 2009. Accessed 5 June 2012. http://www.mckinseyquarterly.com/Motivating_people_Getting_beyond_money_2460.

Morieux, Yves. 'Smart Rules: Six Ways to Get People to Solve Problems Without You'. Harvard Business Review, September 2011. Accessed 4 June 2012. http://hbr.org/2011/09/smart-rules-six-ways-to-get-people-to-solve-problems-without-you/ar/1.

Moss, Mark. 'Sensemaking, Complexity and Organizational Knowledge'. Knowledge and Process Management 8:4 (2001): 217–32.

Muller, Thor and Lane Becker. Get Lucky: How to Put Planned Serendipity to Work for You and Your Business. San Francisco, CA: Jossey-Bass, 2012.

Mullins, Phil. The Polanyi Society, n.d. Accessed 4 June 2012. http://www.missouriwestern.edu/orgs/polanyi/.

Murphy, Rosalie. 'USC's "Senti-meter" Measured Oscar's Social Buzz ... and Predicted Some Winners'. USA Today College, 27 February 2012. Accessed 4 June 2012. http://www.usatodayeducate.com/staging/index.php/ccp/uscs-senti-meter-measured-oscars-social-buzz-and-predicted-some-winners.

Neill, Samuel D. Dilemmas in the Study of Information: Exploring the Boundaries of Information Science. New York: Greenwood, 1992.

Nilsson, Magnus. 'Social Media Analytics Leads to Great Insights and Privacy Concerns'. Magnus Nilsson on Digital Marketing, 19 November 2009. Accessed 5 June 2012. http://www.bravenewme.com/2009/11/social-media-analytics-leads-to-great-insights-and-privacy-concerns/.

Owyang, Jeremiah. 'Explaining What the "Social Graph" is to Your Executives'. Web Strategy by Jeremiah Owyang, 10 November 2007. Accessed 4 June 2012. http://www.web-strategist.com/blog/2007/11/10/what-is-social-graph-executives/.

Papacharissi, Zizi and Maria de Fatima Oliveira. 'Affective News and Networked Publics: The Rhythms of News Storytelling on #Egypt'. *Journal of Communication* 62:2 (April 2012): 266–82.

Pariseau, Leslie. 'Domino's New Campaign: Our Old Pizza Was Bad'. *Slashfood*, 1 June 2010. Accessed 4 June 2012. http://www.slashfood.com/2010/06/01/dominos-new-campaign-our-old-pizza-was-bad/.

Penenberg, Adam L. 'Enter the Pivot: The Critical Course Corrections of Flickr, Fab.com, and More'. *Fast Company*, 5 February 2012. Accessed 5 June 2012. http://www.fastcompany.com/1834196/the-pivot.

Pereira, Daryl. 'Can Twitter Sentiment Analysis Predict Outcomes (Like the Irish Election)?' developerWorks, IBM, 25 February 2011. Accessed 4 June 2012. https://www.ibm.com/developerworks/mydeveloperworks/blogs/business-analytics/entry/can_twitter_sentiment_analysis_predict_outcomes_like_the_irish_election?lang=en.

Perer, Adam. 'Making Sense of Social Networks'. Vimeo, 2011. Accessed 4 June 2012. http://vimeo.com/21298850.

Peter, Laurence J. and Raymond Hull. *The Peter Principle*. New York: W. Morrow, 1969.

Pink, Daniel H. *Drive: The Surprising Truth about What Motivates Us*. New York: Riverhead, 2009.

Pirolli, Peter, and Stuart Card. *The Sensemaking Process and Leverage Points for Analyst Technology as Identified Through Cognitive Task Analysis*. Palo Alto, CA: PARC, 2005.

Pirates of the Caribbean, Dead Man's Chest. Dir. Gore Verbinski. Prod. Jerry Bruckheimer. By Ted Elliott and Terry Rossio. Perf. Johnny Depp, Orlando Bloom, and Keira Knightley. Buena Vista, 2006.

Power, Daniel. 'What is the Impact of Social Media on Decision Making?' Focus.com, 16 April 2011. Accessed 4 June 2012. http://www.focus.com/questions/what-is-the-impact-of-social-media-on-decision-making/.

Pyzdek, Thomas. 'Six Sigma at Motorola'. Quality Digest, December 1997. Accessed 4 June 2012. http://www.qualitydigest.com/dec97/html/motsix.html.

Reichelt, Leisa. 'Ambient Intimacy (FOWA 07)'. slideshare, 5 October 2007. Accessed 4 June 2012. http://www.slideshare.net/leisa/ambient-intimacy-fowa-07.

Ries, Eric. *The Lean Startup: How Today's Entrepreneurs Use Continuous Innovation to Create Radically Successful Businesses*. New York: Crown Business, 2011.

Robischon, Noah. 'WorldBlu's List of Democratic Workplaces Will Make You Want to Work Someplace Else'. *Fast Company*, 14 April 2009. Accessed 5 June 2012. http://www.fastcompany.com/blog/noah-robischon/editors-desk/worldblus-list-most-democratic-workplaces-might-make-you-wish-you-w.

Rogers, Paul, Michael C. Mankins and Marcia Blenko. *Decide and Deliver: Five Steps to Breakthrough Performance in Your Organization*. Boston, MA: Bain & Company, 2010.

Rogers, William. 'Idea Management: Social Workstreams vs. Workflow'. William's Blog, CorasWorks, 30 July 2010. Accessed 4 June 2012. http://solutions-for-sharepoint.com/?p=246.

Rooney, Ben. '"Sentiment Analysis" Aims to Sort Marketing Truths'. *The Wall Street Journal*, 15 March 2012. Accessed 4 June 2012. http://online.wsj.com/article/SB10001424052702304459804577283412417678418.html.

Rosenbaum, Steve. 'Data Through the Ages'. *The Huffington Post*, 21 October 2011. Accessed 4 June 2012. http://www.huffingtonpost.com/steve-rosenbaum/data-through-the-ages_b_1025913.html.

Rosenberger, Larry, John Nash and Ann Graham. *The Deciding Factor: The Power of Analytics to Make Every Decision a Winner*. San Francisco, CA: Jossey-Bass, 2009.

Roth, Craig. 'If You Thought Your Inbox was Overloaded, Wait Until Activity Streams'. Gartner, 8 March 2011. Accessed 5 June 2012. http://blogs.gartner.com/craig-roth/2011/03/08/if-you-thought-your-inbox-was-overloaded-wait-until-activity-streams/.

Ryan, Liz. '10 Jobs that Didn't Exist 10 Years Ago'. *Kiplinger* Personal Finance, 27 January 2011. Accessed 4 June 2012. http://www.kiplinger.com/columns/onthejob/archive/10-jobs-that-didnt-exist-10-years-ago.html.

Sampson, Michael. 'Socialtext 360 Connects Similar Employees'. the brainyard, *InformationWeek*, 17 November 2011. Accessed 4 June 2012. http://www.informationweek.com/thebrainyard/news/social_networking_private_platforms/231903242.

Samuelson, Paul A. and William D. Nordhaus. *Economics*. New York: McGraw-Hill, 1985.

Sanfey, Alan G. 'Social Decision-making: Insights from Game Theory and Neuroscience'. *Science* 318.5850 (2007): 598–602.

Scofield, Deborah Mills. 'Serendipitous Innovation'. *Forbes*, 23 August 2011. Accessed 5 June 2012. http://www.forbes.com/sites/work-in-progress/2011/08/23/serendipitous-innovation/.

Selko, Adrienne. 'Employees First, Customers Second'. *IndustryWeek*, 15 February 2012. Accessed 5 June 2012. http://www.industryweek.com/articles/employees_first_customers_second_26607.aspx.

Semple, Euan. *Organizations Don't Tweet, People Do: A Manager's Guide to the Social Web*. Chichester: John Wiley, 2012.

Shah, Rawn. 'Cooking Up Tasks and Workflows on the Social Web'. *Forbes*, 9 August 2011. Accessed 4 June 2012. http://www.forbes.com/sites/rawnshah/2011/08/09/cooking-up-tasks-and-workflows-on-the-social-web/.

Shah, Sooraj. 'Analysis: What Challenges do Online Retailers Face in 2012?' computing.co.uk, 24 January 2012. Accessed 5 June 2012. http://www. computing.co.uk/ctg/analysis/2141008/analysis-challenges-online-retailers-2012.

Sharma, Nikhil. 'The Origin of DIKW Hierarchy'. Go.webassistant.com, 11 January 2004. Accessed 4 June 2012. http://go.webassistant.com/wa/upload/users/u1000057/webpage_10248.html.

Shirky, Clay. *Cognitive Surplus: Creativity and Generosity in a Connected Age*. New York: Penguin, 2008.

Shirky, Clay. *Here Comes Everybody: How Change Happens When People Come Together*. New York: Penguin, 2008.

Shuaib, Jawad. 'Facebook vs Open Social'. slideshare, 5 February 2008. Accessed 4 June 2012. http://www.slideshare.net/jawadshuaib/facebook-vs-open-social.

Silverberg, Mike. 'Semco: Democracy in the Workplace'. AsOne – Case Study, 14 September 2010. Accessed 5 June 2012. https://www.asone.org/asone/stories/casestudy.html?uuid=c28fbc91-245e-417a-9b35-9bf483b9130c.

Skloot, Rebecca. 'Famous Six Degrees of Separation Study a Fraud?' Science Blogs, 15 January 2009. Accessed 4 June 2012. http://scienceblogs.com/culturedish/2009/01/15/famous-six-degrees-of-separati/.

Sloan, Alfred P. Jr. *My Years with General Motors*. New York: Doubleday, 1963.

Smith, Adam. 'An Inquiry into the Nature and Causes of the Wealth of Nations'. Library of Economics and Liberty, 1904. Accessed 4 June 2012. http://www.econlib.org/library/Smith/smWN.html.

Smith, Cooper. 'The Top 17 Most "Social" Companies'. *The Huffington Post*, 27 July 2011. Accessed 4 June 2012. http://www.huffingtonpost.com/2011/07/27/the-most-social-companies_n_908763.html.

Smith, David. 'Proof! Just Six Degrees of Separation between Us'. *The Guardian*, 3 August 2008. Accessed 4 June 2012. http://www.guardian.co.uk/technology/2008/aug/03/internet.email.

Smith, John David. 'Choosing Social Media for Communities – Mixing Strong and Weak Ties'. slideshare, 28 January 2010. Accessed 4 June 2012. http://www.slideshare.net/smithjd/effat-udec2010v4-6737161.

Solis, Brian. 'Likes, Genre, Action – Facebook Introduces Frictionless Sharing and Actions'. BrianSolis, 25 January 2012. Accessed 4 June 2012. http://www.briansolis.com/2012/01/likes-genre-action-facebook-introduces-clicks-to-action/?utm_source=feedburner.

Solon, Olivia. 'Fiat Releases Details of First Ever Crowdsourced Car'. *Wired UK*, 18 August 2010. Accessed 5 June 2012. http://www.wired.co.uk/news/archive/2010-08/18/fiat-mio.

Spain, William. 'CEO Pay Balloons to 380 times Average Worker's'. *MarketWatch*, 20 April 2012. Accessed 5 June 2012. http://articles.marketwatch.com/2012-04-20/industries/31372105_1_ceo-s-p-line-workers.

Stanley, Marty. 'Best Practices: Transaction vs. Interaction'. *TechJournal*, 29 October 2010. Accessed 4 June 2012. http://www.techjournal.org/2010/10/best-practicestransaction-vs-interaction/.

Suarez, Luis. '5 Reasons Why Activity Streams Will Save You from Information Overload'. socialmedia today, 4 May 2011. Accessed 5 June 2012. http://socialmediatoday.com/luissuarez/292220/5-reasons-why-activity-streams-will-save-you-information-overload.

Surowiecki, James. *The Wisdom of Crowds: Why the Many are Smarter than the Few*. New York: Doubleday, 2004.

Tapscott, Don and Anthony D. Williams. *Wikinomics: How Mass Collaboration Changes Everything*. New York: Portfolio, 2006.

Tassi, Paul. 'EA Shrugs Off Worst Company in America Title'. *Forbes*, 5 Apr. 2012. Accessed 20 June 2012. http://www.forbes.com/sites/insertcoin/2012/04/05/ea-shrugs-off-worst-company-in-america-title/.

Taylor, Peter. *Leading Successful PMOs*. Farnham: Gower, 2011.

Thaler, Richard H. and Cass R. Sunstein. *Nudge: Improving Decisions about Health, Wealth, and Happiness*. New Haven, CT and London: Yale University Press, 2008.

TheSimonSchool. '4th Sands Leadership Lecture'. YouTube, 4 December 2009. Accessed 4 June 2012. http://www.youtube.com/watch?v=EQA0HxGICOg.

Thornhill, Ted. 'Gone in 60 Seconds: 168 Million Emails, 700,000 Google Searches … a Mind-boggling Snapshot of What Happens on the Internet in Just ONE MINUTE'. *Mail Online*, 21 June 2011. Accessed 4 June 2012. http://www.dailymail.co.uk/sciencetech/article-2006091/Number-crunchers-just-happens-60-seconds-internet--A-LOT.html.

Turner, Delaney (ed.). 'IBM Webinar. Beyond the Hype: Using Social Media to Enhance Your Customer Experience'. slideshare, 15 April 2011. Accessed 5 June 2012. http://www.slideshare.net/165yohodr/ibm-webinar-beyond-the-hype-using-social-media-to-enhance-your-customer-experience-7639749.

Van Grove, Jennifer. 'Gamification: How Competition is Reinventing Business, Marketing & Everyday Life'. *Mashable* Social Media, 28 July 2011. Accessed 4 June 2012. http://mashable.com/2011/07/28/gamification/.

Van Grove, Jennifer. 'Google Gets into Market Research, Turns Online Surveys into Paywall Replacements'. VB/Media, 29 March 2012. Accessed 4 June 2012. http://venturebeat.com/2012/03/29/google-consumer-surveys/.

Van Grove, Jennifer. 'SXSW Crowd Earns $10K for Charity by Playing a Game'. *Mashable* Business, 12 March 2011. Accessed 4 June 2012. http://mashable.com/2011/03/12/priebatsch-keynote/.

Weinberger, David. 'The Problem with the Data-Information-Knowledge-Wisdom Hierarchy'. HBR Blog Network, *Harvard Business Review*, 2 February 2010. Accessed 4 June 2012. http://blogs.hbr.org/cs/2010/02/data_is_to_info_as_info_is_not.html.

Weinberger, David. Too Big to Know, 2012. Accessed 4 June 2012. http://www.toobigtoknow.com/.

Wheatley, Malcolm. '67% of Fund Managers Undershoot their Benchmark'. The Motley Fool, 29 November 2011. Accessed 5 June 2012. http://www.fool.co.uk/news/investing/2011/11/29/67-of-fund-managers-undershoot-their-benchmark.aspx.

Woods, Dan. 'Building the Enterprise Social Graph'. *Forbes*, 28 September 2010. Accessed 4 June 2012. http://www.forbes.com/2010/09/27/enterprise-social-media-technology-cio-network-woods.html.

Zeleny, Milan. 'Milan Zeleny – CV & Biography'. Milan Zeleny, 28 September 2009. Accessed 4 June 2012. http://www.milanzeleny.com/?biography.

Zhai, David and Alexis Burson. 'The Ubiquitous Network'. GSAPPonline, Columbia University, 2012. Accessed 4 June 2012. http://www.arch.columbia.edu/work/courses/studio/f10-rothstein/burson-zhai.

Index